WHO GOD SAYS YOU ARE

MUCH LOVE!
MICHELLE
BERKEY
:) ZEPH 3:17

WHO GOD SAYS YOU ARE

LIVE IN THE

Confidence & Freedom

OF YOUR TRUE IDENTITY

Michelle Berkey

❋ GRACE&THE GRAVEL ROAD

COPYRIGHT

DEDICATION

To you who dare hope that God passionately wants to meet you right in the middle of wrong turns you've taken and mud puddles you find yourself in.

This is for you.

Because he does.

FREE AUDIO BOOK!

As a special thank you
for purchasing my book,
I'd love to give you
an absolutely FREE copy of the audiobook!

Go to
www.whogodsaysyouare.link/resources
to access your copy.

RESOURCES

Free stuff is almost as delicious as a dark-chocolate salted caramel. I have a free treat for you! Sadly, not chocolate, but I've put together some free resources that will help you absorb the truths you're about to discover in the following pages. You can access them by entering your email address at: **www.whogodsaysyouare.link/resources**

What you'll find:

✤ Free week of SoulShaper Guided Moments With God (audio sequence)

✤ "How to Meditate on Scripture" (PDF article)

✤ Meditation Verse Printables

✤ "I Am" Printable

✤ "I Am" Affirmation (audio file)

✤ *Who God Says You Are* Audiobook

ARTWORK

Why This Artwork?

Woman: Created is a mixed media collage made to show that we're each a masterpiece specifically designed and brought to life by God. Any discussion of who we are must start and end with this. Let the details of the artwork throughout the book remind you that your identity begins with God's work of creation.

Meditation Verses

I'm not an accomplished letterer, but I've included my own lettered verses in these pages for two reasons. First, lettering is a practice I use to meditate on scripture and so it seemed appropriate. But, more importantly, they're here as a reminder for both you and I that our identity is not in how we perform, how we look to others, or how far along we are on any given journey. Who God says we are is so much bigger, and leaning on those truths takes practice. Like lettering.

CONTENTS

CONTENTS

PREFACE

This book wasn't born because I had some theological arguments to make. It wasn't born because I wanted to increase my influence in the world. This book was born because I'm a perfectionist, a people-pleaser, and a woman going through a midlife identity crisis.

Over ten years ago, I moved across the country to a region with very different values, history, and conventions. I've dealt with a six-year divorce, a bankruptcy, and a business that's grown smaller instead of larger.

Even after rebuilding my life, I didn't know who I was anymore. Perfectionism, workaholism, and people-pleasing had taken a toll on my health and well-being. I wasn't the mom I wanted to be. I wasn't the woman I wanted to be. And, I wasn't the Christ-follower I wanted to be.

I needed a new definition of who I was. My own opinions, experiences, roles, performance, and circumstances weren't enough. They change too easily. I needed something rock-solid. Something I could cling to when circumstances shifted. When divorce papers showed up on my doorstep. When friends failed me.

I began to ask God what it means to be a woman today. Very quickly, I realized I needed to look at something more fundamental than womanhood. I needed to look at personhood first.

Who does God say I am?

I began to dig into the Bible to find out. Then, I decided to take a small group of women with me. We worked through the devotions you're about to read, and we discussed them each Wednesday night. We marveled at God, we saw

new things about ourselves, and we wrestled with unfamiliar—and sometimes uncomfortable—truths. Slowly, my perception of myself changed. I now see myself through the lens of God's Truth more often than the lens of my circumstances, successes, or failures.

This means freedom!

Freedom from living up to impossible standards. Freedom from working to please others. Freedom from fear. Freedom from letting the whims of the economy, culture, or performance power my self-worth.

I want that freedom for you, too!

I want you to understand how precious you are. Not because of anything you've done or accomplished, but because God says that it's true.

HOW TO USE THIS BOOK

You know how to read a book, right? Why would you need instructions?

I have a few reasons for including a "how-to" section in this book. I want to explain what you're going to find in the following pages, give you a few options on how to approach the material, and offer a few tips on getting the most out of it.

How It's Organized

Each of the twelve weeks is divided into seven daily readings:

✠ Day 1: Introduction, prayer and weekly meditation verse

✠ Day 2-6: Devotional readings

✠ Day 7: Summary and prayer

The first and last days of each week are very short, so if you want to treat this as a five-day-a-week devotional, you're easily able to do so. Just tack the first and last days onto your reading on Monday and Friday.

I've included a meditation verse for each week. If you're a memorizer, use it as a weekly memory verse. For those who aren't, here's what I'd like you to do. Go to **www.whogodsaysyouare. link/resources**, enter your email, and find the Meditation Verse Printable in the list of resources. Of course, you're welcome to all the other resources, but right now, the verses are what I want you to focus on.

Download the pdf file and print it. As you come to each week, attach the theme for that week to your mirror, office wall, night table, the inside

of your kitchen cabinet—anywhere you'll see it consistently throughout your day. Read it every time you see it. Use the suggestions in the "How to Meditate on Scripture" article found in the same online resource section to meditate on the verses throughout each week.

How To Read The Devotions

It's easy to treat devotionals like our morning teeth-brushing. We read them, set them aside, and check one thing off our to-do list for the day. We've taken care of our spiritual side and we can now move on to other things, feeling good about ourselves.

Please don't read this book that way!

Life is too uncertain to treat God like a line item on your to-do list. We owe him so much more! The scriptural truths in the following pages are meant for: "teaching, for rebuking, for correcting, for training in righteousness" (1 Timothy 3:16). They're meant to heal broken hearts, call prideful hearts to repentance, encourage the discouraged, save the lost, comfort the broken-hearted, and train us in righteousness.

In short, they're meant to change us.

I need changing. I need the power of God's Word transforming my life into something eternally significant! And, I'm sure you do too!

Here are some suggestions for reading these truths so that they change you:

- Pray before reading each day that the Holy Spirit would speak to your heart as you read, helping you understand and apply the scriptures and concepts to your life..

- Read slowly. Consider the words. Think about them. Savor. Re-read.

✣ Journal or consider your answers to the questions each day when you read, but also throughout your day. Wrestle with them. Struggle.

✣ When you pray the prayer at the end of each day, don't just read it, mean it.

✣ Add your own prayer at the end of the printed prayer. Ask God questions. Unload your sins and grief. Submit yourself to his guidance.

✣ Expect to hear from God. Expect him to speak to you. Yes, even you.

Also, note that the scriptures you'll find in this book are from the *Christian Standard Bible* (CSB) unless otherwise noted.

PRAYER

Father,

I didn't expect this to be a book, but now it is one. These words and stories aren't anything special by themselves, but your Spirit has the power to use them to draw readers closer to you. Please do that! Use what's here to reach into hearts and remind each reader the truth of who they are. Tear away any lies which have lodged there. Transform their lives.

Forgive any errors, sinful motivations, or pride on my part, and let your grace pour out of these pages. Let every reader feel loved, known, and cherished. As they consider each topic, speak a specific message to each reader. Speak love into them. Speak value into them. Speak joy into them. Tell them exactly what you think of them, what you want them to know, and how much you care for them.

Use these words to help all who read them learn to live in the freedom of knowing exactly who you say they are. Use them to do far more than I could ever ask or imagine.

Soli Deo gloria!

I love you. Amen.

INTRODUCTION

Life is uncertain.

What if you believe you are what you do and this Friday afternoon you find out your job has been eliminated?

What if you believe your worth is bound up in your perfect traditional family and you're served divorce papers tomorrow?

What if you believe your parenting is what gives you value and (heaven forbid!) your children are killed in a car accident?

What if you believe your value is found in taking care of everyone around you and you become disabled and no longer capable of caring for yourself, much less anyone else?

What if you believe that your possessions, your address, your alma mater, or your kids' private school explains who you are?

Relying on external circumstances, roles, skills, status, or people as a foundation for your identity will only result in catastrophe. Life is uncertain and circumstances can change in an instant. When you build a foundation on something over which you have no control, and which can change at any moment, you set yourself up for crisis.

Take a few minutes to think about what you've allowed to define you up until today. Words a bully spoke in second grade? An embarrassing moment in middle school? Your family history? Abuse? A sin you just can't get a handle on? What chapters make up the story you tell

yourself about who you are in the dark, quiet hours of the night?

God spends a tremendous amount of time in his Word telling us who we are. What if, instead of external circumstances—what you do, what co-workers or family members think—what if you allow the timeless, unchanging Word of God to define you? What if you build the foundation of your identity on who God says you are?

He's far more trustworthy than your best friend from high school, current boss, or even your spouse. And he has a lot to tell you. *Who God Says You Are* guides you through twelve topics and allows you time to soak in each one. As you read, talk to God, absorb his words, and let them redefine who you are.

If you've ever allowed anything other than God to tell you who you are, this book is for you. If you look to your performance, your roles in life, or your possessions to give you value, this book is for you. If you yearn to live in freedom from catering to what the world thinks of you or expects from you, this book is for you. If you want to re-write the scripts playing in your head to align with the truth of scripture, this book is especially for you.

If you work through each topic and appropriate the truths you read, you will never again believe someone else's story about you. You'll never again allow the world around you to tell you that you're less-than, worthless, small, or forgotten. You'll never again allow the circumstances of life to control you.

You'll live every day in the confidence and freedom of knowing exactly who you are. You will know without a doubt that you are loved.

When you understand who you truly are, it will change everything about how you handle your life. It will eliminate worry and fear. It will allow you to step into all God declares you to be.

Don't stay stuck in the stories other people write for you! Don't stay trapped by your circumstances or your past! God wants so much more for you. The scriptures and concepts you're about to read will transform what you believe about yourself. They will align your beliefs with what God says is Truth.

I can't wait to see how God uses these daily readings to redefine who you are from the inside out! I can't wait for you to experience the freedom that will give you!

Because...

You are not your size.

You are not your work.

You are not your bank account.

You are not your skin color.

You are not your failures.

You are not your successes.

You are not your actions.

You are not your feelings.

You are not your sins.

You are not your depression, anxiety, or mental illness.

You are not your habits.

You are not your past.

You are not your fitness level.

You are not your marital status.

You are not your education.

You are not your ministry.

You are not your disease.

You are not your accomplishments.

You are not your pain.

You are not your family.

You are not your abuse.

You are not your nationality.

You are not your political affiliation.

You are not your group membership.

You are not your lifestyle.

Who are you? Turn the page to begin the adventure of understanding exactly who God says you are.

WHAT'S THE FOUNDATION OF WHO I AM?

WEEK 01

What's the Foundation of Who I Am?

WEEK 01
DAY 01

My son started school this week, and every night he whines about what's going on in the classroom. The teachers are detailing the class rules, setting expectations, and explaining what they'll be teaching this year. My son is not particularly patient with those tactics. He thinks he's heard it all before. He doesn't see the value in reviewing stuff he thinks is unimportant.

When he's older and responsible for providing information for a group of people, he'll understand that it's important to set some norms, help everyone start from the same place, and make sure no one is left behind before they begin. That's what we're doing this week as well. It's tempting to hopscotch right over the basics, but they're critically important. Even if they seem overly familiar, reminding ourselves of these truths is refreshing and renewing to our faith.

This week, we'll think about the following statements:

- I am a sinner.
- I am redeemed.
- I have been purchased with Jesus' blood.
- I am born again.
- I am healed.

PRAY

Father,
I am so guilty of believing my identity and value
comes from my performance, my roles in life,
my work, my service, and my relationships. To
look to these for my sense of self is sin. I'm so
very sorry. Please forgive me. You give me so
many clear indications of who you say I am
in scripture. As we study them in the months
ahead, help me absorb them into my heart.
Help me believe them. Help them become the
foundation of what I believe about myself.

> *Make your ways known to me, Lord;*
> *teach me your paths.*
> *Guide me in your truth and teach me,*
> *for you are the God of my salvation;*
> *I wait for you all day long. (Psalm 25:4-5)*

Help me understand these basic truths of my
relationship with you in a new, deeper, fresh
way this week.

I love you. Amen.

MEDITATION VERSE

Think about this verse throughout the week. Write it on a sticky note and leave it where you'll see it often. Or, go to **www. whogodsaysyouare. link/resources** and download the pdf with the weekly meditation verses. Print and hang the appropriate verse for each week where you'll see it often. Found in the same online resource list, you'll find a guide for meditating on scripture that will explain what it means to meditate on scripture, what it doesn't mean and offer suggestions.

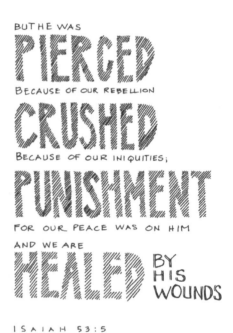

BUT HE WAS

PIERCED

BECAUSE OF OUR REBELLION

CRUSHED

BECAUSE OF OUR INIQUITIES;

PUNISHMENT

FOR OUR PEACE WAS ON HIM

AND WE ARE

HEALED BY HIS WOUNDS

ISAIAH 53:5

WEEK 01
DAY 02

My ex-husband was a custom home builder who created elaborate homes for his clients. Every house started with a set of plans that he and the client developed together. When the plans were finished, it was his responsibility to turn that house from a paper dream into reality. And where did he start? The foundation.

Every area of the country does foundations a little differently. We lived in a fertile, flat area of the Midwest that had easily worked soil. Almost every home had a basement with foundations of poured concrete. Foundations had to be a specific thickness and located at a specific depth. The walls needed perfectly placed openings in the concrete for doors and windows.

The more plumb, or straight, the foundation walls, the easier it would be for all the other subcontractors to do their job well. If the foundation wasn't poured correctly, the house wouldn't fit together as it should. And even if it managed to go together, errors in the foundation would cause trouble in the future. If the foundation isn't made according to safety standards, if it becomes damaged, or is unstable, no amount of fixing on the house above it can correct the problems. With a bad foundation,

fixing cracks or leveling walls above is only a temporary correction. The foundation itself has to be fixed.

As we start this series looking at who God says we are, I want to take a day or two and make sure we get the foundation right. I want us to look at the rest of the study from the right perspective. I no longer live in rural Midwestern farm country. I live in the hills of Middle Tennessee. In my church, we often say that in this area, we are over-churched but under-gospeled. Even if a visitor has been in another church for years, we can't assume they've understood the gospel. Likewise, I won't assume that everyone reading this is a Christ-follower. And, for those of us who are, a fresh reminder of this truth is like a perspective vitamin.

If we're going to understand who we are in Christ and appreciate that position, it's crucial to understand who we are without Christ.

For all have sinned and fall short of the glory of God. (Romans 3:23)

But God proves his own love for us in that while we were still sinners, Christ died for us. (Romans 5:8)

There's a popular belief in the inherent goodness of humanity. And while goodness is certainly present and possible, if you've ever spent significant time around toddlers, you know that we spend much of our time teaching kids how to be good. Not bad. They come out of the womb with that already baked in! We have to train good into their hearts.

None of us is without sin. None. Not me. Not you. Jesus himself is the only exception. This

I Am a Sinner

is the foundation on which we must build our understanding of our identity. This is what we have to understand in order for the rest of the series to make sense.

We are sinners, you and I.

If you are a Christian, meditate on the following verses today and ask God to give you a fresh understanding of the seriousness of your sin.

> *For I am conscious of my rebellion,*
> *and my sin is always before me.*
> *Against you—you alone—I have sinned*
> *and done this evil in your sight.*
> *So you are right when you pass sentence;*
> *you are blameless when you judge.*
> *(Psalm 51:3-4)*

If you are not a Christian or you've realized that you've never understood that you—specifically you—are a sinner in need of a savior, know this:

> *For God loved the world in this way: He gave his one and only Son, so that everyone who believes in him will not perish but have eternal life. (John 3:16)*

Father,

In order for me to understand who I am with

I Am a Sinner

I Am a Sinner

you, I need to be reminded who I am without you. Speak to my heart today about the nature of my own sin. Not my neighbor's, my spouse's or my parent's, but mine. Break my heart over what breaks yours. Let me grieve my sinfulness. Let me understand my inability to perform to your standards and recognize the hopelessness of trying. Send a wave of repentance over me.

I love you. Amen.

WEEK 01
DAY 03

Today, as I stand in my home and look outside, I see miles of snow-covered hills. This would be normal if I lived in the North, but I don't. The Mid-South doesn't get snow like this very often. We're on our fourth snow day in a row, and school has already been called off for tomorrow. This morning I curled up in my comfy rocking chair with my fingers wrapped around a steaming cup of tea as I watched the snow fall.

It was a beautiful thing to watch from the warmth of my home, with nothing critical on my schedule, and the knowledge that I have plenty of food in the house. When we got up this morning, and I took the dog outside in single-digit temperatures, I thought about how dramatically my perception of these snow days is affected by my circumstances.

I see them as lovely breaks from my normal routine. I love having my son at home, and I love the forced slowdown of our busy lives. But if I were homeless and living on the streets of downtown Nashville, my perception of these days would be very different. They would be life-threatening stretches of time during which my only concern would be survival.

Focus on the Family describes a worldview as: "The framework from which we view reality and

make sense of life and the world."[1] If you imagine standing in your home and looking out across snowy hills (or whatever your view might be), the house—the framing, windows, doors, and roof— are the filters through which you view those snowy hills. They're similar to our worldview. You cannot see those snowy fields without your understanding passing through your worldview.

Of course, the analogy isn't perfect. You can step through the door and experience the snow directly. You can inhale the cold air, pack snow into a snowball, and hear the snow crunch underfoot like it does when it's bitter cold. However, you cannot step outside your worldview. So it's critically important that the framework is made up of God's Truth. George Barna says:

> Although most people own a Bible and know some of its content, our research found that most Americans have little idea how to integrate core biblical principles to form a unified and meaningful response to the challenges and opportunities of life.

Our worldview must be driven by what God says about us, not what we think might be true, what our circumstances are, or what our experience has been. When you learn, understand, and apply what God says is the truth about who you are, you can form "a unified and meaningful response to the challenges and opportunities of life."

Yesterday, we laid the first bit of foundational understanding of that truth. Here is the other half of that truth. If your response to the realization that you have a sinful nature is to believe that Jesus Christ was the sacrifice

for your sins, then the Truth of the scripture below forms the framework through which you experience life. This is what God says is true:

> *And when you were dead in trespasses and in the uncircumcision of your flesh, he made you alive with him and forgave us all our trespasses.*
> (Colossians 2:13)

> *Therefore, since we have been declared righteous by faith, we have peace with God through our Lord Jesus Christ.* (Romans 5:1)

> *You are...justified freely by his grace through the redemption that is in Christ Jesus.* (Romans 3:24)

In the weeks to come, we'll unpack more detail about what that means, more nuance. But as we begin, know that at the very basic level, if you are a Christian, God says that the penalty required by your sin has been paid by someone else; Jesus.

- If you are honest, what percentage of your worldview is made up of God's Truth?
- What circumstances, accumulated beliefs, and opinions make up the rest?
- How should believing your identity (in simplest terms) to be a "sinner saved by grace" affect your behavior and your life?

I Am Redeemed

Father,

I know that the framework of my worldview and my beliefs about myself are riddled with the opinions of others, the effects of my culture, and the pride of my own thoughts. Forgive me. Help me get rid of all of that untruth in the weeks to come. Help me see myself the way you do. Help me rebuild the framework with the Truth of scripture. Help me learn, understand, absorb, and apply what I learn in the following pages. Transform my beliefs and my life through these scriptures in a lasting, life-altering way.

Today, let the truth that I am a sinner saved by grace permeate my thoughts and my behavior.

I love you. Amen.

WEEK 01
DAY 04

My son is a Boy Scout. One of the (many) things he needs to do for his next rank advancement is to decide on something he wants to buy (This is never a problem for him.), make a plan to earn the necessary money, adjust the plan if needed, earn the money, compare prices from at least three locations, and make the purchase.

The point of this exercise is to teach the scouts the value of work and effort, that money and, therefore, buying power is the end result of effort, of the wisdom in shopping around, the experience of delayed gratification, and the satisfaction of the process.

He's thinking about working toward a $30 video game. As I think about that, I'm struck by how little he sees $30 to be. At his age almost 40 years ago, I viewed $30 as a lot more. In reality, it was a lot more. In 1978, $30 had the buying power of $121 today.[2] Money fluctuates in value.

For you know that you were redeemed from your empty way of life inherited from your fathers, not with perishable things like silver or gold, but with the precious blood of Christ, like that of an unblemished and spotless lamb. (1 Peter 1:18–19)

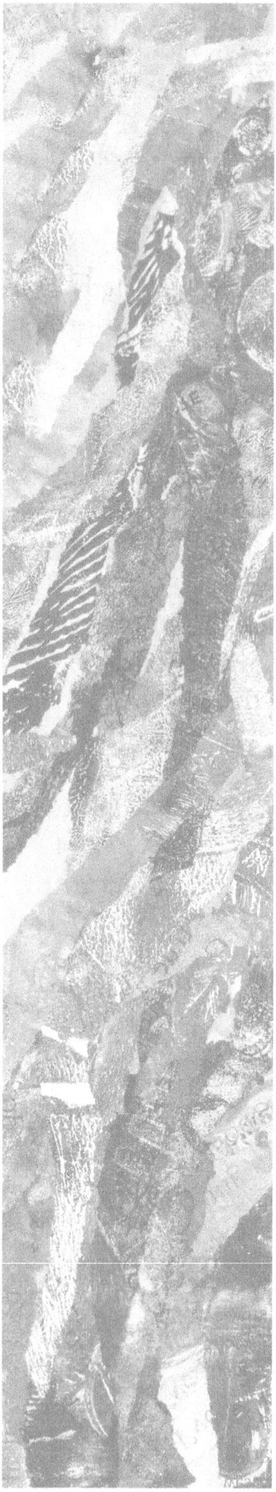

I Am Purchased with Jesus' Blood

The word "redeem" means "to buy out." In Hosea 3, the Lord tells Hosea to find his adulterous wife, Gomer, and love her again. Can you imagine the level of emotion packed into all sides of that command? Gomer had probably sold herself into slavery. Obediently, Hosea went and purchased his wife. He bought her out of sin back into a loving relationship. He redeemed Gomer.

Christ redeemed you as well. The use of that specific word, "redeem," means that before purchase you were a slave (to sin). What I've been thinking about today is what we were purchased with: "...not with perishable things like silver or gold, but with the precious blood of Christ."

The blood of Christ is not a perishable thing. It's never going to disappear. It's never going to change in value like the paper my son needs to earn for his purchase.

Your blood is of utmost value to you. The blood of Christ is of utmost value to God. That's what was spent to redeem you from slavery. It's not dependent on a government for its value. It's enduring. Permanent. Eternal. Of infinite value. Precious.

- What does the fact that Christ's blood is not perishable mean for you?
- What does the preciousness of the blood of Christ say about you?
- How does this affect how you see yourself?

I Am Purchased with Jesus' Blood

Father,

That you see me as so valuable to exchange your son's blood for me is astonishing to me. I don't see myself as that valuable. But you have said it is true. So help me to believe it. Help me understand deep in my bones so that it would permeate all of my thoughts about myself. I am precious enough for you to intentionally redeem me from slavery by the blood of your son. And that permanent, enduring, precious, imperishable blood ensures that purchase for all eternity. Thank you for the finality of this purchase. Thank you for declaring my value in such terms. May it transform my perception of my own value.

I love you. Amen.

WEEK 01
DAY 05

Birth is a painful process. Especially for the mother.

The baby gets squeezed, forced into the bright light and harsh realities of a new world. But the pain belongs to the mom. Mom does the work. I admit I had it relatively easy. From the time my water broke to my son's birth was about five hours. I pushed hard for about an hour. Did it hurt? Yes. Was it worth it? Oh, most definitely, yes!

In John chapter 3, Jesus was speaking to Nicodemus. Nicodemus was a very religious man. He was a Pharisee, a "ruler of the Jews." He did lots of religious stuff. Everyone knew him as a religious guy. He recognized that Jesus was from God. But he was confused by Jesus' statements.

Jesus replied, "Truly I tell you, unless someone is born again, he cannot see the kingdom of God." "How can anyone be born when he is old?" Nicodemus asked him. "Can he enter his mother's womb a second time and be born?" Jesus answered, "Truly I tell you, unless someone is born of water and the Spirit, he cannot enter the kingdom of God." (John 3:3-5)

The only way to enter the kingdom of God

is to be born a second time. This isn't a simple metaphor. If you've always thought of it as a word picture, it's not. It's a spiritual reality. As a mother suffers the pain in a physical birth, Christ suffered so that we might be born a second time, a birth of the Spirit. While becoming a Christian is in some ways a choice on your part, God does the work. Simply reciting a prayer does not accomplish your salvation. God does that. He births you into a new creation.

> *...because you have been born again—not of perishable seed but of imperishable—through the living and enduring word of God.* (1 Peter 1:23)

My eleven-year-old nephew died unexpectedly a few months ago. This month, my ex-husband was in the hospital for a few weeks with, essentially, kidney failure. Medication has restored his kidney function, but there were some very touch-and-go days. Physical birth inevitably leads to physical death. The "seed of man" is perishable. It's a reality of this human existence that you and I will both die.

But the second birth, the spiritual birth, is by imperishable seed. Jesus Christ existed before time and will always exist. He accomplishes your spiritual birth. There is no end to this new creation like there is with physical birth.

Your spiritual birth is a reality, not a word picture, and God accomplished it for you.

❖ Why would it be important to understand

your spiritual birth as a true event, a spiritual reality rather than a metaphor?

✤ Have you experienced the second birth Christ speaks of?

Father,

Help me absorb this understanding. It's hard sometimes for me to understand spiritual reality as real because I can't see or touch it. But I know it is more real, more true, more lasting, more important than my eyes that are reading this prayer. Help me live my life, go through today, respond to my surroundings, but especially respond to you, with the recognition of that fact. Thank you for doing the work of my spiritual birth. Thank you for voluntarily suffering so that my second birth could be accomplished. Thank you for loving me.

I love you. Amen.

WEEK 01
DAY 06

Have you ever tripped over an open dishwasher? I have. It hurts. A lot! My mother did it the other day, and she has a pretty big lump on her ankle and a monster—and I do mean monster—bruise on her chest where the upper rack broke her fall.

My best friend is in treatment for stage-four cancer. This week I spent several hours with a friend who has pneumonia, and one of my son's close friends had emergency brain surgery this week. This flu season is worse than it's been in a decade and is expected to last into summer.

Everywhere I turn, I see the need for physical healing. Scripture is littered with accounts of Jesus physically healing those with lameness, blindness, sicknesses, demon possession, leprosy, and other diseases.

Jesus went into Peter's house and saw his mother-in-law lying in bed with a fever. So he touched her hand, and the fever left her. Then she got up and began to serve him. When evening came, they brought to him many who were demon-possessed. He drove out the spirits with a word and healed all who were sick, so that what was spoken through the prophet Isaiah might be fulfilled:

He himself took our weaknesses
and carried our diseases. (Matthew 8:14-17)

Very early in the morning, while it was still
dark, he got up, went out, and made his way
to a deserted place; and there he was praying.
Simon and his companions searched for him,
and when they found him they said, "Everyone
is looking for you."
And he said to them, "Let's go on to the
neighboring villages so that I may preach
there too. This is why I have come."
(Mark 1:35-38)

Physical healing is a wonderful thing. But
spiritual healing is more important. He may
choose to heal us physically. But the healing we
all need more is spiritual. Jesus healed many one
night, but the next morning, when many more
were looking for him, he suggested they get back
to what he really came for: spiritual healing.

We all went astray like sheep;
we all have turned to our own way;
and the Lord has punished him
for the iniquity of us all. (Isaiah 53:6)

...so that what was spoken through the
prophet Isaiah might be fulfilled:
He himself took our weaknesses
and carried our diseases. (Matthew 8:17)

It's much less obvious than our need for
physical healing, but you and I both need
spiritual healing. Jesus has done that for us.

But he was pierced because of our rebellion,
crushed because of our iniquities;

punishment for our peace was on him,
and we are healed by his wounds. (Isaiah 53:5)

It's very easy to get wrapped up in our physical needs and ignore our spiritual needs. Hear me—physical needs are important. I won't minimize that reality. There are too many people around me with serious physical needs right now to think otherwise.

But Jesus prioritized spiritual healing. And so must we.

- When you think about your own needs, what do you tend to prioritize?
- What physical healing do you need right now?
- What spiritual healing do you need right now?
- How can you learn to focus on the eternal rather than the temporary?

Father,

Give me a heart full of gratitude for the spiritual healing you've given me. Heal me in spiritual ways I don't even know I need and heal me in the physical ways I'm very aware of. Help me value the eternal over the temporary.

I love you. Amen.

WEEK 01
DAY 07

This week we've covered some foundational aspects of who God says we are. We recognized that we're sinners, redeemed, purchased by the blood of Jesus, born again, and spiritually healed.

What has God spoken to your heart this week?

How have these truths changed the way you think or feel about yourself?

Father,

Thank you for making a way for me to be in a relationship with you. I thank you that I can rely on the blood of Christ as permanent and unchanging. Thank you for the spiritual truths that I've been through a new birth and have been spiritually healed. Keep making these truths more and more real to me.

I love you. Amen.

Next week, we'll look at what these truths mean for you in a legal sense. Did you know there was a legal component of your relationship with Christ?

WHAT'S THE LEGAL BASIS FOR WHO I AM?

WEEK 02

WEEK 02
DAY 01

It's ridiculously easy to find different opinions about politics and morals on social media. We all seem to have strong opinions about what our laws should be and what acceptable behavior looks like. Even though we often disagree about them, we understand that there are appropriate behavioral standards for decent human beings, while community, state, and national laws must also exist to govern a society. These two standards aren't always the same, but most people would agree that they both exist.

We looked at moral standards last week. This week we're going to be considering what God says about the legal aspects of our identity. We'll think through the following statements:

✤ I am not condemned.

✤ I am free from sin's power.

✤ I belong to God.

✤ My sins are forgotten.

✤ I am sanctified.

What's the Legal Basis for Who I Am?

PRAY

Father,

Open my understanding of your words this week. Help me grasp clearly my spiritual legal standing and how that should affect my beliefs, my attitudes, and my behavior.

I love you. Amen.

MEDITATION VERSE

Think about this verse throughout the week. Write it on a sticky note and leave it where you'll see it often. Or, go to **www.whogodsaysyouare.link/resources** and download the pdf with the weekly meditation verses. Print and hang the appropriate verse for each week where you'll see it often. Found in the same online resource list, you'll find a guide for meditating on scripture that will explain what it means to meditate on scripture, what it doesn't mean and offer suggestions.

THEREFORE,
THERE IS NOW
NO CONDEMNATION
FOR THOSE IN CHRIST JESUS
BECAUSE
THE LAW OF THE SPIRIT OF
LIFE IN CHRIST JESUS,
HAS SET YOU FREE
FROM THE LAW OF
SIN AND DEATH.

ROMANS 8:1-2

WEEK 02
DAY 02

Larry Nassar is a former USA Gymnastics team doctor. In 2017, he pleaded guilty to charges of child pornography and was sentenced to 60 years in prison. In late 2017, he entered a guilty plea to 10 counts of sexual assault. In January of 2018, he was sentenced to serve 40-175 years after the 60-year federal prison term is fulfilled. He was abusing children under the guise of medical treatment; children who were seeing him to relieve pain and improve their health. More than 150 women have accused Nassar of sexual abuse.[1]

It's pretty easy for us to look at this story and see the legal component. Nassar was breaking federal laws and has been found guilty and sentenced for crimes he committed. But there's also a moral component.

Listening to the women confront Nassar during the sentencing hearing was heartbreaking. News reports and social media feeds were full of coverage and editorials about this story, which is said to be one of the largest sexual abuse scandals in sports history.[2] The public is outraged because it's morally reprehensible to use, damage, and abuse young girls the way he did.

Our standing with God has both a legal and

moral component as well. We spoke of the moral component last week when we talked about the spiritual sickness of sin for which we all need Jesus' healing. God says you are healed.

Sin also presents a legal problem. You've broken God's law, and the punishment for sin is death. You're legally under the sentence of spiritual death. But, the good news of the gospel means that Christ's righteousness is credited to you, and you cannot be condemned for the crimes you've committed.

> *Therefore, there is now no condemnation for those in Christ Jesus, because the law of the Spirit of life in Christ Jesus has set you free from the law of sin and death. (Romans 8:1-2)*

No condemnation. Someone else took the sentence and punishment that you deserve, and you are released from the requirements of the law. This, my friends, is beautiful, life-giving, soul-drenching grace.

It's as if after sentencing, someone stepped up before the judge and offered to serve Larry Nassar's sentences; offered to be condemned in his place. That didn't happen in the courtroom last week for Mr. Nassar. But spiritually, it's available for him through Jesus Christ, just as it is for you. You might not be convicted of multiple counts of child abuse, but we are all guilty under God's law.

But because Jesus died in your place, you are not condemned.

I Am Not Condemned

✣ Have you chosen to accept Christ's payment for your sins?

✣ What is your reaction today to the grace of God given to you?

✣ How does your freedom from condemnation cause you to want to live?

Jesus,

I'm so moved by your choice to take my punishment. It wasn't an easy, pain-free path you chose in obedience to the Father. It was excruciating and lonely. Thank you for doing that for me. Help me be always reminded of the beautiful, sacrificial, loving nature of that precious gift. Help me live, speak, act, and worship in ways that reflect the truth of the freedom you've given me. In gratitude and love for that freedom. In the reality of my "no condemnation" legal standing. Bring to my heart ways that my attitudes and actions need to change to align with that truth.

I love you. Amen.

WEEK 02
DAY 03

I have a very good friend who's been through some serious emotional trauma in the past year and a half. She's been a Christian since she was a teenager and has always had one of the most tenacious relationships with God I've ever seen.

The storms that have crashed into her life recently were devastating and dark. I'm not talking about your garden-variety dark. Garden-variety dark ruins lives daily. No, I'm talking about serious dark where evil has come out to play and isn't subtle about it. She's emerged from that storm now, and she's starting to heal, starting to rebuild her life.

We talked recently about how she felt during this season. She's been angry at God. Her trust was destroyed. She felt hopeless, and abandoned.

For sin will not rule over you, because you are not under the law but under grace. (Romans 6:14)

John Piper explains,

> Being "under grace" means being out from under wrath. And when we are out from under the wrath of God, all his power stands in the service of his mercy to help

do whatever it takes to get us to glory (Romans 8:30). So the first answer is: being under grace guarantees that sin will not be master over us because being under grace means being out from under wrath, and having all the power of God on our side and not against us.[3]

We're affected by the sins of others, and we still have a sin-nature in ourselves. But, we are no longer ruled by sin. Without Christ, we live under the law—the rules God put in place. When we're trying to live up to the law's requirements, we have to drum up our own righteousness. We must be perfectly able to fulfill every tiny portion of that law at all times.

We can't.

As Christians, we realize this and we accept the sacrifice of Christ on the cross for our failures to meet the standard of perfection.

But it's so easy to still act as if our righteousness earns us something. We act as if our service, our attendance at church, our consistency in prayer or Bible study earns us points with God. As if he loves us more when we're doing a laundry-list of good deeds. But if we want to provide any of our righteousness as proof of our worthiness to God, we have to provide all of it. We can't do that. We absolutely must depend on Christ's righteousness instead, for all of it.

My friend is a fighter. She's never been weak. She's weathered more storms in her life than any two people I know combined. And yet, this almost undid her. As she thought back over the last year, she realized that while she was feeling hopeless and abandoned by God, she was not.

She now sees his hand in every moment. She sees his care for her and guidance of her life at every turn. What felt far more real at the time, though, was that the darkness was overwhelming and in charge.

> *Be sober-minded, be alert. Your adversary the devil is prowling around like a roaring lion, looking for anyone he can devour.* (1 Peter 5:8)

Sin is not like a domesticated pet with a mean streak. God says sin is like a roaring lion. A wild animal, vicious, seeking your complete destruction. The good news is that if you're "under grace" you are no longer under the sovereignty of sin. Sin is no longer the ruler of your heart. Sin no longer has the final say. The darkness no longer controls your destiny. God does.

✤ Do you have moments when you've felt far from God? Abandoned? Angry? Overcome by darkness or sin?

✤ What do you now understand is the truth about those moments?

✤ When God's Word and your feelings do not agree, which is true?

✤ How can this help you?

I Am Free From Sin's Power

Father,

Sin is a real thing. So much more real than I often give it credit for. Maybe "real" isn't exactly what I mean. Maybe it's that I recognize it as real, but not as dangerous as it is. Give me a true perspective on sin. But let me always understand that it no longer has the final say in my life. I choose to allow Christ's righteousness to be the basis for my standing before God. Help me recognize when I fall back into false thinking. Let me understand myself as free from the power of sin over my life, and let me live that way. Help me recognize and repent of the times when I'm trying to earn your approval by my own performance.

I love you. Amen.

WEEK 02
DAY 04

I have a crazy Boxer dog. Well, he's not really crazy anymore. Or, at least not as often. When I first brought him into my home, he was a foster pup, and I was called because he'd been in five different homes in six months, and the family that had adopted him was returning him to the rescue I worked with. He'd destroyed drapes and part of a home. He'd gotten into a fight (I prefer to think of it as a minor disagreement.) over food at a doggie daycare, so he was no longer welcome there. He routinely escaped a backyard with a six-foot fence (The boy has a serious vertical jump.), and the owner just couldn't deal with it anymore.

I went to pick him up, took one look, and I was smitten. I brought him home, provided shelter, regular meals and water (something he had not always had), and consistent behavior guidelines, training, and a high degree of control. Over the last few years, he has been transformed from crazy to (mostly) calm. It's typically now one of the first things people remark about when they meet him. They marvel at what a calm personality he has.

A few months after I brought him into my home, long before he got anywhere near calm, I

purchased him from the rescue. I bought him. I handed the rescue organization my hard-earned cash and he became mine. I paid for a troubled dog. He was still trouble, you see. I was working with him, guiding him, training him, and loving him, but he was still tilting far more toward crazy than calm. But I loved him.

I have owned him now for about four years, and today he's generally a bouncy (I said mostly calm, remember?), well-adjusted pup who makes a wonderful pet. It was a long road getting here, and he's had several serious relapses requiring emergency calls to my professional dog-trainer friend. There are a number of analogies that arise from my relationship with him, and we may revisit them later in this series. But for today, here's what's relevant.

I loved him. I bought him. He's now mine. He's microchipped so that I can be identified as his owner by any vet in the country. I made the effort to purchase him, and his legal status has changed. He belongs to me.

> ...*for you were bought with a price. So glorify God with your body.* (1 Corinthians 6:20)

> *You were bought at a price; do not become slaves of people.* (1 Corinthians 7:23)

God loves you and went to the effort to purchase you by the sacrifice of his son on the cross. His blood purchased you into his ownership and you now belong to him.

You were bought with a price. There are ramifications of that purchase. The scriptures above lead to how we're to respond to that knowledge. But today, let's just sit with the idea that the Creator of the universe loved you and

purchased you. Your spiritual legal status has changed. You belong to him.

- What emotions does the idea that God purchased you bring up?
- What does it say about your value and worth?
- How does your life today reflect God's ownership?

Father,

If I think about paying the life of my son for something, that thing would have to be of infinite value. I can't imagine trading his life for anything on this earth. But you did that for me; you gave up the life of your son to purchase me. And, like I purchased my pup before he was well-behaved, you purchased me while I was still in rebellion to you. You love me. And I'm so grateful for that. I'm so amazed that you would ascribe to me that kind of value. But you did. And you do. Help me absorb the truth of that. Help me understand that the way you see me and the way I see me are often so different. When my feelings don't match up with your truth, your truth wins. You find me valuable enough to pay the price of your son's life. And I love you.

Amen.

WEEK 02
DAY 05

I routinely forget where my keys are. I don't usually really lose them; they're just very often temporarily misplaced. I lost my glasses the other day and had to put my contacts in to find them. It's hard to look for something when you can't see well. I frequently walk into a room or up the stairs and forget why I'm there.

I forget these details far more often when my schedule is overloaded, or I'm mentally or emotionally overwhelmed.

We usually think of forgetting in negative terms. But have you ever thought about what a powerful thing forgetting can be?

What if you forgot the laundry list of shortcomings you hold against your parents, best friend, or spouse?

What if you forgot the story you tell yourself about why you're not good enough?

What if you forgot the betrayal you felt or the hurts you've received?

What would life be like if you chose to forget some of those things?

It would be like magic, the release we could provide ourselves if we could choose to forget specific things.

We can, you know. It can be difficult, and you may have to do it more than once. You may have

to keep choosing it over and over. But you can choose to forget.

How does God treat your sins when you have
accepted Christ's payment for them?
and I will never again remember
their sins and their lawless acts.
(Hebrews 10:17)

He chooses to forget them. He chooses not to remember your lies. He chooses not to remember your prideful, self-serving attitude. He chooses not to remember your drunkenness, rebelliousness, affairs, and addictions. He chooses never again to remember them.

What an amazing gift! I'm certain that you have a much harder time choosing to forget them than God does, but in his perfection, if he chooses to never again remember them, why should you dwell on them? He doesn't just forget the small stuff. He chooses not to remember all of your sins—the big stuff, too.

He promises never to remember them again.

✤ How do you think about your own sins? Do you remember them frequently? Diligently? Consistently? Intentionally?

✤ What thoughts or feelings do you have about God choosing not to remember your sins?

✤ How does God's choice not to remember your sin affect your choices about remembering them?

My Sins Are Forgotten

Father,

I'm kind of overwhelmed at the idea of how much I'm living with my own sin at the forefront of my thoughts. That, while I've repented and walked away from it, I'm still stuck in it—though you've long-since forgotten it and choose never to remember it again. You choose never to remember it. Why am I dwelling on it? If your sacrifice was enough to make me clean, why should I keep mucking around in guilt in my head? If your sacrifice was enough to make me clean, what more can feeling bad do for me? I'm awed at your grace and love toward me. Thank you for choosing to never again remember. Thank you for the gift of freedom that brings. For the lifting of guilt and shame. Thank you, Jesus, for your sacrifice that makes that possible. And thank you for choosing me.

I love you. Amen.

WEEK 02
DAY 06

As I'm writing today, I just received a message from our school system that in light of the recent Florida school shooting, and the fact that there have been 18 school shootings in the last six weeks, school is closed on Monday. Our students will not be reporting to school on Monday, but teachers, staff, and law enforcement will be gathering to review and revise the emergency preparedness plans in the district. Rather than school as usual, Monday will be set apart for what's essentially a safety summit.

I'm planning on leaving town on Monday morning and heading to the beach. My parents have become snowbirds and invited me to join them for a week. Free beach vacation? Count me in! It was a bit difficult to find a week that I could leave; I hadn't scheduled it far enough in advance. But I managed. Rather than business as usual, next week will be set apart for some planning, refreshment, and working seaside.

> *And some of you used to be like this. But you were washed, you were sanctified, you were justified in the name of the Lord Jesus Christ and by the Spirit of our God.*
> *(1 Corinthians 6:11)*

"Sanctification" is a translation of the Greek

word "hagiasmos," meaning "holiness" or "set apart," according to Strong's Concordance. Sanctification means to be set apart for God, for his purposes. At the time we become believers, we're immediately granted a positional holiness in Christ. This is also called justification.

There is also a progressive sense of sanctification. The Holy Spirit works in us to guide us toward maturity, a "practical, progressive holiness"[4] during our lifetimes. When our lives are finished here on earth, we'll be forever free from the power of sin and be fully sanctified, or glorified.

You're set apart for God. You're free from sin's authority, being made progressively more free from the power of sin as you allow the Holy Spirit to work in your life, and, ultimately you will be fully sanctified in God's presence.

I've set apart next week's beach trip on my calendar as holy to the Lord—I mean, as worthy of my worship—wait, I mean, as a much-needed break. Positionally on my calendar, I've set it apart to relax. But I'll become progressively more relaxed as the week passes and, (ideally) by the end of the week, be in full-on beach bliss. Which is ultimately where the analogy falls apart, because it's a working vacation, and that fully-relaxed state is probably a pipe dream for this trip. But your positional justification, progressive sanctification, and ultimate glorification in the presence of God is a rock-solid guarantee.

I Am Sanctified

- What are some examples you see of your progressive sanctification? Are you maturing in your faith?

- How does the Holy Spirit accomplish this in your life?

Father,

Thank you for all the work you've done for me. Thank you for creating me, for having a purpose for me, and for refining me toward that purpose. I give free reign to your Spirit to continue to work in my life. Mature me. Grow me up, spiritually. Bring me ever closer to your heart, ever deeper in relationship. Create a hunger in me for spiritual growth.

I love you. Amen.

WEEK 02
DAY 07

This week we've covered some legal aspects of who God says we are. We've considered the truths that we are not condemned, we are free from sin's power. We belong to God, and our sins are not just forgiven, but they're forgotten. We are sanctified.

What has God spoken to your heart this week?

How have these truths changed the way you think or feel about yourself?

Father,

We've covered some heavy, complicated, theological concepts, words, and truths this week. Help me absorb the message(s) you have for me from those concepts. Plant them deep in my heart and let them grow into a sense of self that aligns with your Word.

I love you. Amen.

Next week we'll begin a few weeks of focusing on our spiritual relationship status. How does our relationship with God define us?

WHAT'S MY RELATIONSHIP STATUS? PART 1

WEEK 03

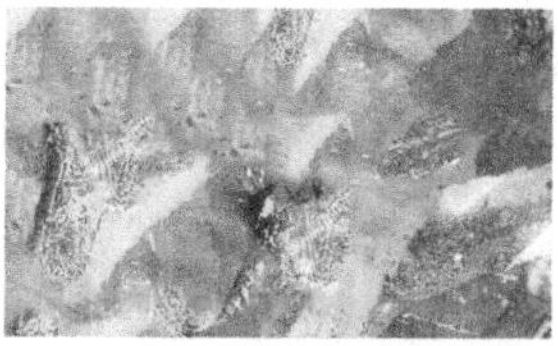

What's My Relationship Status? Part 1

WEEK 03
DAY 01

We can reach out and touch our family and friends. We can look into their eyes, lean on their shoulders, and hug them until they squirm out of our grasp. Not that I've ever done that to anyone!

Relationships with the people around us, we understand. But what does a relationship with God really mean? What does God say our relationship status is, and how does that affect who we believe we are?

This week, we'll consider the following declarations:

- I am dependent.
- I am loved.
- I am chosen.
- I am adopted.
- I am a child of God.

PRAY

Father,

Human relationships—all the relationships I've ever known—are full of the tendency of people to sin. I've experienced hurt, betrayal, and pain right alongside love, generosity, and friendship. But my relationship with you is different, because you are different.

You say I am beloved, and it is always and forever the truth.

You say that you have chosen me and I can trust that will always and forever be the truth.

In the next few weeks, help me understand who I am through the way you've described our relationship. Transform the way I see myself to align with the way You see me.

I love you. Amen.

MEDITATION VERSE

Think about this verse throughout the week. Write it on a sticky note and leave it where you'll see it often. Or, go to **www.whogodsaysyouare.link/resources** and download the pdf with the weekly meditation verses. Print and hang the appropriate verse for each week where you'll see it often. Found in the same online resource list, you'll find a guide for meditating on scripture that will explain what it means to meditate on scripture, what it doesn't mean and offer suggestions.

"THOUGH THE MOUNTAINS MOVE AND THE HILLS SHAKE MY LOVE WILL NOT BE REMOVED FROM YOU AND MY COVENANT OF PEACE WILL NOT BE SHAKEN," SAYS YOUR COMPASSIONATE *Lord*

ISAIAH 54:10

WEEK 03
DAY 02

Years ago, I read an article that compared nations and ranked them on a spectrum of how highly they value community versus individuality. Not surprisingly, the United States had one of the highest rankings in the world for valuing individualism. Americans are more likely than even Europeans (who share many of our national values) to prioritize individual liberties and believe that we shape our own destiny.[1] We are groomed from infancy to place an incredibly high value on self-reliance and individualism.

In July 2012, author and blogger Chris Guillebeau asked his audience on Facebook and Twitter what independence means to them. Here's a handful of their answers:

🟰 You don't answer to someone else.

🟰 You determine your own schedule, values, and priorities.

🟰 You stand alone.

🟰 Being able to depend upon yourself.

🟰 Self-reliance.[2]

I can't help but believe that these answers, this cultural bias toward self-reliance, make it harder

to value the dependence that I need to embrace in my relationship with Christ.

A spiralizer recently took up residence alongside my rice maker and food processor in the gadget cabinet in my kitchen. Last night, I made chicken with pesto zoodles. It was so good and so simple that I got brave and made oven-baked, wavy, spiral potato chips tonight. I bought potatoes this afternoon, and when it came time for dinner, I cut the ends off to attach to my spiralizer. These potatoes were just purchased today; they looked beautiful. Not like sprouted, soft spuds that have been sitting around waiting for something to do for a few weeks. They were firm and unblemished. But when I sliced into them, they were full of black spots on the inside.

We handle so much. We're skilled, talented, and competent. We've learned how to change diapers, provide for our families, and make noodles out of vegetables. Rosie the Riveter says, "We can do it," and we agree. We have so much of our lives under control. Or, rather, the semblance of control. But like the rotten potatoes I brought home today, the facade of control masks a different reality.

We really can't control very much at all. When the veneer is cut away by chance or circumstance, we're faced with the reality that our ability to control anything is limited. We need God. In those moments, dependence grows. When our lives fall apart, when the unexpected happens, and when circumstances overwhelm us, dependence flourishes, because we're forced to acknowledge our need. Divorce papers, job losses, death, accidents, cancer diagnoses. These things destroy the facade of our self-sufficiency. We turn to God for help and

cling to him.

But he doesn't want us to depend on him only when we're at the end of our own resources. He wants us to depend on him when we feel like we can handle life on our own as well. In 2 Chronicles 16, King Baasha went to war with King Asa of Judah. Earlier, King Asa relied on God for military victory. But this time, he had his own plans and resources. He thought he could handle this attack with a human alliance, rather than depending on God. And it worked. Or, so he thought. God wasn't pleased.

> At that time, the seer Hanani came to King Asa of Judah and said to him, "Because you depended on the king of Aram and have not depended on the Lord your God, the army of the king of Aram has escaped from you. Were not the Cushites and Libyans a vast army with many chariots and horsemen? When you depended on the Lord, he handed them over to you. For the eyes of the Lord roam throughout the earth to show himself strong for those who are wholeheartedly devoted to him. You have been foolish in this matter. Therefore, you will have wars from now on." (2 Chronicles 16:7-9)

It's very easy to rely on ourselves when we think we have the resources to handle life. But just because we can doesn't mean we should. That's a parenting phrase you should apply to your own life regularly. I'm in a constant battle to do just that right now as I prepare to launch a business. God wants us to use our talents and gifts. We should act. But we should depend on God rather than our own resources and plans.

Dependence is a daily battle, privilege, and joy.

I Am Dependent

✤ How has your cultural background or experiences biased you toward or away from the idea of dependence on others?

✤ Does this bleed over into your relationship with God?

✤ How does the idea that you are utterly dependent on God feel to you?

✤ What characteristics of God become important to you in thinking about your dependence on him?

Father,

Forgive me for my constant slip into self-reliance. Help me not think of my dependence on you as a weakness. Help me understand the truth of your Word. Help me know so very deep in my heart that my dependence is centered in your completely trustworthy, completely loving, completely powerful, completely "for-me" nature.

I love you. Amen.

WEEK 03
DAY 03

My Dearest Friend,
...should I draw you the picture of my heart it would be what I hope you would still love though it contained nothing new. The early possession you obtained there, and the absolute power you have obtained over it, leaves not the smallest space unoccupied.

I look back to the early days of our acquaintance and friendship as to the days of love and innocence, and, with an indescribable pleasure, I have seen near a score of years roll over our heads with an affection heightened and improved by time, nor have the dreary years of absence in the smallest degree effaced from my mind the image of the dear untitled man to whom I gave my heart.[3]

~ Abigail Adams to John Adams

...The charms of the incomparable Josephine kindle continually a burning and a glowing flame in my heart...I thought that I loved you months ago, but since my separation from you I feel that I love you a thousand fold more. Each day since I knew you, have I adored you more and more.[4]

~ Napoleon Bonaparte to Joséphine de Beauharnais

I Am Loved

Dearest Angel Girl:

...I suppose most of us are lonely in this big world, but we must fall tremendously in love to find it out. The cure is the discovery of our need for company—I mean company in the very special sense we've come to understand since we happened to each other—you and I. The pleasures of human experience are emptied away without that companionship—now that I've known it; without it joy is just an unendurable as sorrow. You are my life—my very life. Never imagine your hope approximates what you are to me. Beautiful, precious little baby—hurry up the sun! Make the days shorter till we meet. I love you, that's all there is to it.[5]

~ Orson Welles to Rita Hayworth

Happy Birthday Princess. We get old and get used to each other. We think alike. We read each others [sic] minds. We know what the other one wants without asking. Sometimes we irritate each other a little bit. Maybe sometimes take each other for granted. But once in a while, like today, I meditate on it and realize how lucky I am to share my life with the greatest woman I ever met. You still fascinate and inspire me. You influence me for the better. You're the object of my desire, the #1 earthly reason for my existence. I love you very much.[6]

~ Johnny Cash to June Carter

Dearest Heart,

...And when the wind blows and the rains fall and the sun shines through the clouds (as it is now) he still resolves, as he did then, that nothing so fine ever happened to him or anyone else as falling in love with Thee—my

dearest heart.[7]

~ President Richard Nixon to First Lady Pat Nixon

*The Lord appeared to him from far away.
I have loved you with an everlasting love;
therefore, I have continued to extend faithful
love to you. (Jeremiah 31:3)*

*As the Father has loved me, I have also loved
you. (John 15:9a)*

*Father, I want those you have given me to be
with me where I am, so that they will see my
glory, which you have given me because you
loved me before the world's foundation.
(John 17:24)*

*For rarely will someone die for a just person—
though for a good person perhaps someone
might even dare to die. But God proves his
own love for us in that while we were still
sinners, Christ died for us. (Romans 5:7-8)*

*For God loved the world in this way: He
gave his one and only Son, so that everyone
who believes in him will not perish but have
eternal life. (John 3:16)*

*This hope will not disappoint us, because
God's love has been poured out in our hearts
through the Holy Spirit who was given to us.
(Romans 5:5)*

*Now this is what the Lord says—
the one who created you, Jacob,
and the one who formed you, Israel—
"Do not fear, for I have redeemed you;*

I have called you by your name; you are mine."
(Isaiah 43:1)

"Though the mountains move
and the hills shake,
my love will not be removed from you
and my covenant of peace will not be shaken,"
says your compassionate Lord. (Isaiah 54:10)

For I am the Lord your God,
who holds your right hand,
who says to you, 'Do not fear,
I will help you.' (Isaiah 41:13)

You did not choose me, but I chose you.
I appointed you to go and produce fruit
and that your fruit should remain, so that
whatever you ask the Father in my name, he
will give you. (John 15:16)

And remember, I am with you always, to the
end of the age. (Matthew 28:20b)

~ Jesus Christ to you

I tend to think of God's love toward me in an intellectual sense. I understand that he has love toward me. But it's not simply an intellectual idea. He loves me—and you—with a never-ending, raw, deeper than we can imagine, fierce, tender, emotional love.

✤ Have you considered before that the Bible is God's love letter to you? Have you read it that way?

✤ Earthly loves aren't perfect, but Jesus is. How does that encourage you?

✤ How does being beloved of God change how you see yourself?

Father,

You just love me. I want to say I'm not worthy of it...but of course, I'm not, and my worth has nothing to do with your love for me. Help me understand that at a deep, deep level. Thank you so very much for your love. Remind me that it's far more than an intellectual idea. Remind me that it's emotional, and I love you.

Amen.

WEEK 03
DAY 04

I wasn't much of a doll girl growing up. But I did have a lot of stuffed animals. A lot of stuffed animals—but only one favorite. A koala bear named "Kwala." Pretty original, I know. My sister and I would set up schools for our favorite bears to learn in. We enjoyed making the books and desks and school things more than we actually enjoyed playing school with the bears.

There was nothing particularly special about our bears. Mine was partly stuffed and partly a bean bag, and I liked the way the bean part felt. He looked similar to other bears; he wasn't made of fancy fur, didn't have valuable eyes. Mostly, he was special because he was mine. Because I chose him.

Scripture tells us repeatedly that God chose us.

For he chose us in him, before the foundation of the world, to be holy and blameless in love before him. (Ephesians 1:4)

You did not choose me, but I chose you. (John 15:16a)

You are a chosen race, a royal priesthood, a holy nation, a people for his own possession. (1 Peter 2:9a)

John Piper explains:

> If you have believed on Jesus, the wonder is that you were first appointed to eternal life. You weren't appointed because you believed; you believed because you were appointed. When the Gentiles heard that the gospel actually included them, "they began rejoicing and glorifying the word of the Lord, and as many as were appointed to eternal life believed." (Acts 13:48)
>
> Revel in the wonder that you are a Christian because God chose you to be one. Your roots, as a child of God, are in eternity—in the infinite mind and heart of God. Your faith, and all its fruit, are God's eternal gift.[8]

God chose you.

You were not chosen because you could offer something special to God.

You were not chosen because you were well-behaved or read your Bible consistently.

You were not chosen because you were exceptionally lovely. Or lovable.

In the same way, then, there is also at the present time a remnant chosen by grace. (Romans 11:5)

Grace is the basis on which you were chosen. And that means you never have to live up to a performance, a measuring stick, or a standard to stay chosen. Relax into that idea today. God chose YOU.

I Am Loved

❖ Do you tend to believe there are reasons why God chose you based on who you are? Or what you do?

❖ How does this affect your spiritual health?

❖ What does the idea that God chose you based on his own love and grace imply about who you are?

Father,

You chose me. I don't know why, but I am yours. Thank you for the gift of that grace-soaked choice. Thank you for not resting that decision on my own worthiness. Thank you for the privileges that come with that choice. Help me realize the depth of your grace so that I can share it with others as generously and as easily as breathing.

I love you. Amen.

WEEK 03
DAY 04

Scrolling through Facebook this morning, I came across a video story of an adoptive family. A respiratory nurse at a hospital became the mother of an infant who had been abandoned and found by a local teenager in a truck bed. That baby spent a period of time abandoned, cold, wet, and, no doubt, scared. He had no future. If not found, he had no way to fend for himself, protect himself, or provide for himself. He would have died of exposure or starvation. Instead, a week later, he was heading home from the hospital with a new family.[9]

His new family consisted of a mother who was a two-time survivor of breast cancer, a father, and the father's three grown children.[10] This new family would now be legally responsible to care for that infant in every way. He would have every legal right as his new siblings. He could now be embraced by his new family as one of their own. The child had been legally, physically, and emotionally transformed from no hope to a bright future. It was a beautiful story.

You're in the same spiritual state as this infant boy in the truck bed.

You did not receive a spirit of slavery to fall back into fear. Instead, you received the Spirit

of adoption, by whom we cry out, "Abba, Father!" (Romans 8:15)

The nature of adoption is parents choosing—both as an act of will and an expression of love—to bring a child into their family forever. To choose to bear the responsibility, cost, risks, emotions, and time investment in that child. To give the child a family name, a home, and a future. That's a huge decision; a generous, love-drenched choice.

That's exactly what God has done for you. He adopted you into his family, bore the cost for your redemption at the cross, took the risk of being grieved by your decisions, gave you his name, made continual investments in your growth, and designated you to be an heir of his kingdom. And he does this all with great love. This isn't just a legal or technical reality. It's an expression of divine love.

John Piper describes God's heart for adoption:

> Adoption in God's mind was not Plan B. He predestined us for adoption before the creation of the world. Plan A was not lots of children who never sin and never need to be redeemed. Plan A was creation, fall, redemption, adoption so that the full range of God's glory and mercy and grace could be known by his adopted children. Adoption was not second best. It was planned from the beginning.

God chooses to love you and adopt you into his family because it pleases him to do so. And, now you can call him "Daddy" in the nature of a child addressing a perfectly loving father.

✤ What is your perspective on adoption? Do you see adoption as a "nice thing some people do"? As a means to grow a family when biological children are not an option? Or as a beautiful reflection and expression of the gospel?

✤ What does your spiritual adoption mean to you? That you were a child with no future and now are the member of a family with full privileges and a relationship to the creator of the universe as "Abba"?

✤ How does your adoption affect the way you understand who you are?

Abba, Daddy,

I'm chosen and loved as a full member of your family. You lavish on me the privileges of a son when my birthright is chaos and sin. Let me understand in a new way today the depth of love that brought me into that family. Share your heart for adoption with me and help me understand and experience my true place in your family.

I love you. Amen.

WEEK 03
DAY 06

I have wonderful parents. This week, I'm writing from a sun-drenched top-floor bedroom of a cottage overlooking the Gulf of Mexico. I'm able to do that because my parents are here for the month of February and asked me to join them for a week. There are privileges that go along with being the daughter of my parents! I don't have a perfect family, certainly. But I had a safe, secure, and happy childhood. Many don't.

Over 140 million children worldwide are orphans.[11] My brief research suggests that this number is woefully underreported. The International Labour Organization reports that worldwide, there are 152 million who are child laborers, accounting for almost 11% of children.[12] Almost half of all deaths of children aged newborn through five are related to malnutrition.[13] Almost half of all people living in extreme poverty are children, although they only make up approximately a third of the world's population.[14]

Clearly, I had it pretty good. Clearly, children are an at-risk population.

Before knowing Christ, you were a spiritual orphan, at-risk, with the spiritual poverty,

homelessness, fear, and vulnerability that often comes with being an orphan.

> *But to all who did receive him, he gave them the right to be children of God, to those who believe in his name.(John 1:12)*

> *For all those led by God's Spirit are God's sons. You did not receive a spirit of slavery to fall back into fear. Instead, you received the Spirit of adoption, by whom we cry out, "Abba, Father!" The Spirit himself testifies together with our spirit that we are God's children, and if children, also heirs—heirs of God and coheirs with Christ—if indeed we suffer with him so that we may also be glorified with him. (Romans 8:14-17)*

As children of God, we are the members of God's household.

As children of God, we experience the intimacy of the parent/child and family relationships.

As children of God, we have the security of God's protection and provision.

As children of God, we are his heirs.

As children of God, we have been freed from a life of fear.

As children of God, we grow to resemble our Father.

As children of God, we are subject to our Father's authority and discipline.

As children of God, we are dependent on our Father.

As children of God, we have a Father perfect in every way, who loves us perfectly.

I Am A Child of God

✤ Which of these statements is easiest for you to relate to? Why?

✤ Which of these statements is most difficult for you to relate to? Why?

✤ What do you feel is most important about being a child of God?

Abba, Daddy,

Help me not take my status as your child lightly. Help me understand its privileges and responsibilities in new ways today. Increase my intimacy with you and the rest of my spiritual family. Help me grow into a family resemblance. Help me appreciate your discipline and increase my dependence on you. Thank you for adopting me as your child.

I love you. Amen.

WEEK 03
DAY 07

This week, you've soaked in the ideas that you are dependent on, loved, chosen, adopted by, and a child of God.

How would you describe your relationship status today?

What has God spoken to your heart this week?

How have these truths changed the way you think or feel about yourself?

Father,

The words that you use to describe us—loved, chosen, adopted—are so much more than I deserve. They're beautiful expressions of how much you care for me. Help me understand them at the core of my being. Build them into a rock-solid foundation in my life. Reveal areas where I don't honor that position in our relationship. Draw me deeper and deeper into a love relationship with you.

I love you. Amen.

Next week, we'll begin a second week of focusing on our spiritual relationship status.

WHAT'S MY RELATIONSHIP STATUS? PART 2

WEEK 04

WEEK 04
DAY 01

We have some beautiful truths in store for us this week! You'll be amazed at the ways God describes you!

This week we'll think about these statements:

✜ I am a daughter of the King.

✜ I am a friend of Jesus.

✜ I am a slave.

✜ I am a saint.

✜ I am a member of Christ's body.

PRAY

Father,

A daughter of God? A friend of Christ? A saint? These aren't terms that come to mind when I'm thinking about who I am. But they should. Help me understand them this week and open my heart to what you want me to know. Destroy any lies you find in what I believe about myself.

I love you. Amen.

MEDITATION VERSE

Think about this verse throughout the week. Write it on a sticky note and leave it where you'll see it often. Or, go to **www. whogodsaysyouare. link/resources** and download the pdf with the weekly meditation verses. Print and hang the appropriate verse for each week where you'll see it often. Found in the same online resource list, you'll find a guide for meditating on scripture that will explain what it means to meditate on scripture, what it doesn't mean and offer suggestions.

FOR *we* ARE GOD'S *masterpiece* HE HAS CREATED US ANEW IN *Christ Jesus* SO WE CAN DO THE *good things* HE PLANNED FOR US LONG AGO.

EPH. 2:10

WEEK 04
DAY 02

I was born between Disney princesses. I grew up later than the classics like Cinderella and Sleeping Beauty. But I was too old for the next round. I was graduating college when Ariel ushered in the parade of princesses that would take the '90s by storm. I didn't even have daughters as an excuse to watch them. And I've only had boys, leading to further insulation from the princess culture.

However, I did come of age during the engagement and marriage of the real-life princess, Diana, Princess of Wales. I remember marveling at her wedding. Many girls of my generation were enthralled with the romance of marrying into the royal role of princess. Not me. I remember watching the wedding and being struck by the weight of it. The weight of history, expectations, rules, and responsibilities—not to mention the dress!

You see, while a princess has all the advantages of a royal household (which are nothing to sneeze at), she also has the responsibility of a regal rank. Kathy Howard explained it well when talking about Grace Kelly's marriage to Prince Rainier of Monaco:

When Grace Kelly married the Prince

of Monaco she entered a life of privilege and royalty. Yet with it came great responsibility. She was expected to produce an heir to the throne. She had to leave things from her previous life behind. No more acting for Kelly, in fact, the Prince banned her movies in Monaco. Kelly was no longer Grace the actress, she was Princess Grace, wife of the ruler of Monaco and the mother of the heir to the throne. She was the representative of her people and her country to the world. She had to act like the princess she was.[1]

For he chose us in him, before the foundation of the world, to be holy and blameless in love before him. He predestined us to be adopted as sons through Jesus Christ for himself, according to the good pleasure of his will. (Ephesians 1:4-5)

The moment you accept Christ's sacrifice for your sins, you become a member of the household of God. But, not just any member. Not an indentured servant. Not a distant relative. You are God's child. You're a princess, the daughter of the King. Did you catch that? You have a royal rank. You're honest-to-goodness royalty!

I've never understood the fascination with princesses. Had Ariel, Belle, and Jasmine fueled my childhood, maybe my opinion would be different. But why (given the choice of gender-appropriate royal rank) wouldn't you choose queen? Yes, more responsibility, but also more power. More potential.

Several years ago, I was on a girl's weekend trip in the Blue Ridge Mountains of North Carolina, and I bought each of us silver crown magnets

as souvenirs. Each has a different word on it. I wrapped them and let each girl choose one at random, and I kept the one that was left.

The one on my refrigerator says, "princess." I've always been uncomfortable with it.

Thinking about it today, though, I'm so very glad to hold the rank of a princess, to be a daughter of the King. Should I want to be queen instead, as I've always thought? As Eve tried to wrest control of her own destiny from the hand of God, so my preference for choosing to be queen is a demand for independence and control. Instead, I need to foster a submitted spirit. A dependence on my Father. Not the independent, self-directing spirit already so front-and-center in my nature.

...but our citizenship is in heaven, and we eagerly wait for a Savior from there, the Lord Jesus Christ. (Philippians 3:20)

As a princess, I have the privileges of a beloved royal daughter. But I also represent my Father, the King, to the world, and I need to act accordingly.

✛ As a Christian, you are by definition a daughter of the King. What does this realization mean to you?

✛ What privileges does it afford you? What responsibilities does it entail?

✛ How well do you live your life as a representative of your heavenly citizenship?

I Am a Daughter of the King

✤ Is there an action you need to take after answering these questions?

Father,

Help me understand who I am as a daughter of the King. Help me internalize the privileges and responsibilities that result from that relationship. Help me live well as a representative of your kingdom.

I love you. Amen.

WEEK 04
DAY 03

Twelve years ago, I agreed to meet a new acquaintance for lunch. We sat down to eat our salads and immediately connected. I vividly remember looking her in the eyes and saying, "I have plenty of acquaintances and not a lot of free time. I'm interested in more friendships that go deeper than talking about the weather and why our kids don't do exactly what we tell them to. If you'd like that, I'd love to be real friends." She immediately agreed, leading to years of rich friendship.

A woman I love dearly walked through the dark days of my divorce with me. She fed me every weekend, took care of my son when I needed a break, and loved on me in extraordinarily practical and useful ways. Her food, conversations, and gentle care kept me sane through six years of emotional chaos during my divorce and bankruptcy.

I have friends who are unwaveringly supportive of all of my crazy projects and endeavors. They're my biggest fans and they're always actively cheering me on, even when they shake their heads. But I usually interpret that as amazement at what a great idea it is.

I have a friend I call when my rescued dog goes berserk and destroys his crate (Yes, this

has happened more than once.). I also have friends who watch my son when I need to travel, friends who talk me off the ledges of anxiety and depression, friends who don't care if my house is a mess, friends who cry with me and pray with me, friends who go adventuring with me, friends who hold me accountable, friends who call me out on stupid moves or bad decisions. These friends feed my body and my soul.

And I do the same for them.

- Friends really listen.

- Friends love unconditionally and forgive easily.

- Friends speak the truth, whether it's easy or difficult.

- Friends are helpful, loyal, and encouraging.

- Friends have seen you at your worst and still love you.

- Friends enjoy your company.

- Friends celebrate your wins and support you during losses.

- Friends share joy and fun.

- Friends often know you better than you know yourself.

- Friends make sacrifices for you.

- Friends stick with you through good times and bad.

I could go on for a few pages like this, but you probably already know these things, and you could make a list just as easily.

I Am a Friend of Jesus

I do not call you servants anymore, because a servant doesn't know what his master is doing. I have called you friends, because I have made known to you everything I have heard from my Father. (John 15:15)

Let that sink in a moment. The Creator of the universe calls you his friend. Jesus chose you as his friend.

- Take a look at the "Friends..." list above. Consider how each item applies to the friendship you have with Christ.
- How does the idea that Jesus chose you as a friend change how you see yourself?
- What is one way you can be a better friend to Jesus?

Father,

Why would you choose me as a friend? Why me? You tell me that you designed me to display your glory. I know you love me. Speak into my heart today the truth of what you see in me.Teach me what it means to be a friend of yours. Help me cherish our friendship, develop our friendship, and honor our friendship.

I love you. Amen.

WEEK 04
DAY 04

A few months ago, after being told he was allowed to paint only in the yard, my son spray-painted a Nerf gun part on a piece of cardboard on our patio. It was raining and he decided the cardboard was enough protection for the cement. It might have been—had it been larger than a macaroni-and-cheese box! Not only had he disobeyed a direct order, but now we had to figure out how to get graffiti off the cement.

As a result of this little walk on the rebellious side, he was going to have to put in some extra time working around the house. I claimed my right to anything I wanted of him, and I uncharacteristically posted on Facebook that he was my slave for the next week. In the post I asked for advice to remove the paint, and I mentioned there would be both hard work and random silliness required to fulfill this role. He was going to work hard, but there would be moments of fun as well. An acquaintance took serious offense at my post. She sent me a private message describing how insensitive I was to use the term "slave," and that she expected better of me.

I wasn't going to be using my son in an abusive way. And I certainly didn't mean to disparage the

very real plight of people enslaved across the world. Maybe I was using the term a bit lightly, but here's the very real truth. We are all slaves. You are a slave. I am a slave. My son is a slave. The woman who scolded me is a slave.

One of the definitions of "slave" is "a person who is excessively dependent upon or controlled by something." We tend to object to the idea of being a slave, either because of cultural connotations or the lack of freedom it implies. But we as humans are divided into two categories: sinners and saved sinners. As sinners, we are controlled by our own desires. What we desire most controls our behavior, whether that's money, pleasure, or anything else. As saved sinners, we still have sinful desires, but we don't serve them. We serve Christ.

Don't you know that if you offer yourselves to someone as obedient slaves, you are slaves of that one you obey—either of sin leading to death or of obedience leading to righteousness? But thank God that, although you used to be slaves of sin, you obeyed from the heart that pattern of teaching to which you were handed over, and having been set free from sin, you became enslaved to righteousness. I am using a human analogy because of the weakness of your flesh. For just as you offered the parts of yourselves as slaves to impurity, and to greater and greater lawlessness, so now offer them as slaves to righteousness, which results in sanctification. For when you were slaves of sin, you were free with regard to righteousness. So what fruit was produced then from the things you are now ashamed of? The outcome of those

things is death. But now, since you have been set free from sin and have become enslaved to God, you have your fruit, which results in sanctification—and the outcome is eternal life! For the wages of sin is death, but the gift of God is eternal life in Christ Jesus our Lord. (Romans 6:16-23)

Who or what enslaves you? If you're a believer, it's very easy to answer "Christ" without much thought. Because you're "supposed to." But dig a little deeper today. Consider the attitudes, fears, influences, and beliefs that control your behavior. What enslaves you?.

- What things have enslaved you in the past?
- What things enslave you today?
- How is being a slave of righteousness evident in your life?.

Father,

I'm so grateful for your gift of eternal life, for freeing my life from slavery to sin. Help me to live in a way that reflects my slavery to righteousness. Build into me obedience and a hunger and thirst for your Word and your ways. A heart that knows that its master is called "Abba" and "I Am". Make me a willing, humble, eager servant of Christ.

I love you. Amen.

WEEK 04
DAY 05

Have you ever looked up a word in the dictionary and found the printed definition to be just flat-out wrong? Of course not! The dictionary has been the source of word knowledge my whole life. Scrabble games have been won or lost by it. Arguments have succeeded or failed based on it (What, doesn't your nerdy family argue over words?!). Term papers have been graded by it.

Like the constitution is to our government, the dictionary is a foundational document to a writer. The word-realm runs on the engine of the dictionary. Sure, our language is fluid and there are always new words and new uses of old words. But the dictionary is never just flat-out wrong.

Until today.

Today, I looked up a word we use in the church. I understand the biblical definition. I understand the Catholic Church uses the term differently than I read it in the New Testament. And I was curious what the dictionary said. I feel like my foundation has been shaken. The dictionary is not infallible. Or, at best, incomplete.

The word I'm talking about is "saint." Culturally, we agree with the dictionary. Here's what it says:

noun

1. a person acknowledged as holy or virtuous and typically regarded as being in heaven after death.

2. used in titles of religious saints.

verb

1. formally recognize as a saint; canonize.[2]

The Catholic Church has a series of requirements before sainthood is given to someone as a title, including death, investigations into a person's life and theology, and verified miracles attributed to his or her intercession.[3]

Maybe this has influenced the culture and the definition above, because we tend to think about a saint as someone with a high degree of holiness.

Extra-good. Extra-righteous. A+ on the holiness grading curve. A saint (in the general sense, not the officially-canonized sense) is someone who sets the bell curve of righteousness for the rest of us.

But is that how Paul used the term in his letters? At the beginning of his letters to the Ephesians, Philippians, Corinthians, and Colossians, he addresses his remarks to "the saints." These are letters to church people. Everyday-messed-up-sinful-but-forgiven church people. The same kind of people who sit next to you on Sunday. Exactly the same kind of person who sat in your spot the last time you attended church.

You are a saint.

I Am a Saint

That's not a statement of the quality of your life or your attainment of virtue. It's not a reflection of the number of miracles you've performed or the streak you're on for the number of days in a row you've prayed. Rather, it's a description of your spiritual status.

To the church of God at Corinth, to those sanctified in Christ Jesus, called as saints, with all those in every place who call on the name of Jesus Christ our Lord—both their Lord and ours. (1 Corinthians 1:2)

A saint is a person "set apart to be Christ's own possession."[4] We don't often use the word "saint" the way Paul did, but we should.

We need to be reminded every day and in every way that we have been set apart and belong to Christ. Every believer is a saint. Former prostitutes. Former thieves. Former adulterers. Those who struggle with doubt, pride, or selfishness. Me. You.

⁜ What has the word "saint" meant to you?

⁜ How does it feel to call yourself a saint?

⁜ What difference would a biblical use of the word "saint" mean in the life of your church? Your family? Your heart?

I Am a Saint

Father,

I understand that I don't need to achieve a particular degree of holiness to be a saint, but I sometimes forget that. Remind me on a regular basis that it's not my actions that define my sainthood, it's your action. Sink the idea that you have called me a saint, that you set me apart for your own purposes deep into my heart.

I love you. Amen.

WEEK 04
DAY 06

It's late summer as I write this, the first week of August. We're still melting in the heat, the kids are going back to school, and I noticed this week that it's getting darker earlier in the evening. I noticed it because I have a headlight out. After I realized why I couldn't see the road, I remembered that it's been burned out since spring. I haven't been driving in the dark for a long time, so I'd completely forgotten about it.

It's a small little part, that driver's-side low-beam headlight bulb. Laying next to a fuse, a steering column, and a battery on a workbench, it wouldn't do much of anything. Wouldn't look impressive. Wouldn't have any purpose. But plugged into the exact right place with the roughly 30,000 other parts that make up a car, it allows me to drive my son safely home from a scout meeting after dark. Pretty amazing when you think about it.

It might be small, but it was missed. Did we make it home without it? Yes. Did the car still work? Yes. But it would have worked better if that particular piece had been functioning like the manufacturer intended.

All of you together are Christ's body, and each of you is a part of it. (1 Corinthians 12:27 NLT)

I Am a Member of Christ's Body

When you become a Christian, you are placed into the body of Christ in a particular place, with an individual mix of gifts, and a perfectly-designed-specifically-for-you purpose.

For we are God's masterpiece. He has created us anew in Christ Jesus, so we can do the good things he planned for us long ago.
(Ephesians 2:10 NLT)

Years ago, my teenage stepson was caught shoplifting a reel of fishing line. Thankfully, he chose to pocket that unpaid-for item in a store with a particularly strict policy on shoplifting. The police were called and he was put through the wringer, barely escaping prosecution. That $1.14 joyride didn't seem quite so worth it by the time he got home four hours later, emotionally exhausted.

What did I do then? I packed the whole family up in the car, and we drove to both sets of grandparents and an aunt and uncle's house. At each home he had to explain the incident and apologize in person. Why? Because we're part of a family and our actions and choices affect the other members of our family.

Our relationship with God changes when we choose to accept Christ's sacrifice for us. But that's not the only relationship affected. We also gain a family. We're placed into the body of believers with a purpose. An individual purpose that contributes to the overall purpose of the group.

How you choose to mature as a Christ-follower, obey God, and develop your gifts affects all of us. It affects the purpose of the church. Whether you have been designed as the

human equivalent of a low-beam driver's-side headlight bulb or a battery, you matter. You were created and gifted for specific things that God has planned for you.

Together, we make up the body of Christ as all the parts make up my Subaru Forester. They work together to make the car accomplish its purpose. Together for us is sometimes harder than together for auto parts. While sometimes they break, they're not selfish, sinful, independent, or full of pride as a Christ-follower. And their job is not as critical as ours.

You are a member of the body of Christ. You matter. You have a purpose. And your actions, attitudes, and obedience affects all of us.

✤ Do you believe you have an important role as a member of Christ's body? Why or why not?

✤ How do your actions and behaviors reflect that belief?

✤ Does your belief align with God's Word?

✤ What's one belief, attitude, or action affecting your spiritual family that needs to change?

Father,

It's really easy to think that our actions, beliefs, and attitudes are private, that we don't affect others, but we do. You say we're all part of a

I Am a Member of Christ's Body

body, all interconnected. Help me see myself as part of a whole. Help me understand at a really deep level that you created me for a very specific purpose, and help me learn what that is. Thank you for providing a spiritual family for me. Help me learn how to be a healthy, contributing member of that family.

I love you. Amen.

WEEK 04
DAY 07

This week, we've looked at what God says about our relationship with him. He says that you are a daughter of the King, his friend, a slave, a saint, and a member of Christ's body.

What has God spoken to your heart this week?

How have these truths changed the way you think or feel about yourself?

Father,

The word pictures, the analogies, and the descriptions you've given us are beautiful. I'm so grateful that you've spelled out in so much detail who you, as my Creator, say I am. Help me to believe it at a heart and soul level. Help that belief affect my attitudes and behaviors. Make it real to me.

I love you. Amen.

Next week, we'll tackle a confusing term. What does it mean to be "in Christ"?

WHERE AM I AND
WHY DOES IT MATTER?

WEEK 05

WEEK 05
DAY 01

"In Christ" is an odd phrase, but so important to understand as a Christ-follower. We need to understand what "in Christ" means so that we can live from that place. This week, we'll examine these statements:

✛ I am in Christ.

✛ I am alive in Christ.

✛ I am a new creation.

✛ I am connected.

✛ I am complete in Christ.

PRAY

Father,

We're going to look at how you've positioned us in Christ this week, and as we do, I ask that you make scripture come alive to me. Guide me into a deeper relationship with you. Help me understand the enormity of what you've done for me and how that affects my identity. Work to make my perspective of who I am align with your perspective.

I love you. Amen.

MEDITATION VERSE

Think about this verse throughout the week. Write it on a sticky note and leave it where you'll see it often. Or, go to **www.whogodsaysyouare.link/resources** and download the pdf with the weekly meditation verses. Print and hang the appropriate verse for each week where you'll see it often. Found in the same online resource list, you'll find a guide for meditating on scripture that will explain what it means to meditate on scripture, what it doesn't mean and offer suggestions.

*H*E MADE THE ONE
WHO DID NOT KNOW SIN
TO BE SIN FOR US
SO THAT IN HIM
WE MIGHT BECOME
the righteousness of God

2 COR 5:21

WEEK 05
DAY 02

Many years ago, I took a road trip to the Northeast. It was the first time I'd driven through Vermont, New Hampshire, and Maine. I remember the awe I felt as we traveled a part of the country I'd never seen before. I stopped at each scenic overlook and gawked in amazement at the beauty of the rocky coast and rugged mountains.

That lasted about two days.

Soon, I stopped pulling off at every overlook. I got choosier about whether a stop was interesting enough to warrant the effort. By the end of the week, I was rarely pulling off to look. When I did, I didn't stay very long. I no longer stared out the windows non-stop. What happened in that week? The view didn't change. It was just as stunning as it had been a few days before. But my perception of it did. It became familiar. Commonplace. It's so easy to become immune to the beauty around you.

The same thing happens with the basics of our faith. We read the term "in Christ" or "in Christ Jesus" in a scripture passage and we forget what a stunning statement that is. It's not just another term for being a Christian.

It is from him that you are in Christ Jesus, who became wisdom from God for us—our

righteousness, sanctification, and redemption.
(1 Corinthians 1:30)

God positions you in Christ when you become a believer. It's his action, not yours (although you've participated by accepting Christ's sacrifice on your behalf). Let's look at an analogy of what that means from another passage.

"I am the true vine, and my Father is the gardener. Every branch in me that does not produce fruit he removes, and he prunes every branch that produces fruit so that it will produce more fruit. You are already clean because of the word I have spoken to you. Remain in me, and I in you. Just as a branch is unable to produce fruit by itself unless it remains on the vine, neither can you unless you remain in me. I am the vine; you are the branches. The one who remains in me and I in him produces much fruit, because you can do nothing without me." (John 15:1-5)

The gardener (God) has made us to be the branches connected to the vine (Christ). This isn't just a description of a position. It's a vital, living relationship. You and Christ are connected. You share in his life through this connection. You are in him.

What do you share? Each of the following verses contains the phrase "in Christ" or "in Christ Jesus." Read through them slowly with a fresh perspective. Stop at the scenic overlooks. Wonder at what God has done for you and given you

....according to his own purpose and grace,

which was given to us in Christ Jesus before time began. (2 Timothy 1:9b)

For he chose us in him, before the foundation of the world, to be holy and blameless in love before him. (Ephesians 1:4)

For the wages of sin is death, but the gift of God is eternal life in Christ Jesus our Lord. (Romans 6:23)

For just as in Adam all die, so also in Christ all will be made alive. (1 Corinthians 15:22)

For I am persuaded that neither death nor life, nor angels nor rulers, nor things present nor things to come, nor powers, nor height nor depth, nor any other created thing will be able to separate us from the love of God that is in Christ Jesus our Lord. (Romans 8:38–39)

In him we have redemption through his blood, the forgiveness of our trespasses, according to the riches of his grace. (Ephesians 1:7)

He made the one who did not know sin to be sin for us, so that in him we might become the righteousness of God. (2 Corinthians 5:21)

Therefore, if anyone is in Christ, he is a new creation; the old has passed away, and see, the new has come! (2 Corinthians 5:17)

...for in Christ Jesus you are all sons of God, through faith. (Galatians 3:26 ESV)

He also raised us up with him and seated us with him in the heavens in Christ Jesus. (Ephesians 2:6)

For all the promises of God find their Yes in

him. (2 Corinthians 1:20 ESV)

To the church of God at Corinth, to those sanctified in Christ Jesus. (1 Corinthians 1:2)

And my God will supply all your needs according to his riches in glory in Christ Jesus. (Philippians 4:19)

And the peace of God, which surpasses all understanding, will guard your hearts and minds in Christ Jesus. (Philippians 4:7)

- What implications does the understanding that you are in a vital, connected relationship with Christ have for your life?
- Which of the "in Christ" verses resonates with you most today and why?

Abba, Daddy,

You've established a living connection with me. Your Holy Spirit lives inside me. I'm not at arm's length; you are with me. Give me a fresh perspective to wonder today at the amazing gifts you've given me in Christ. May I never, ever, become so accustomed to them that I fail to feel awe at your provision for me.

I love you. Amen.

WEEK 05
DAY 03

I've started writing this several times. I'm not sure why it's so difficult! All my writing is difficult right now. I go through cycles of depression, and it may be that one of them has snuck up on me.

I'm sure that everyone who struggles with depression experiences it somewhat differently. For me, it feels hopeless. I feel completely worthless and like I'm dead inside. Things that usually bring me joy or delight no longer do and my thought patterns are noticeably different. It seems to affect my perspective of my identity particularly powerfully.

And you were dead in your trespasses and sins in which you previously lived according to the ways of this world, according to the ruler of the power of the air, the spirit now working in the disobedient. We too all previously lived among them in our fleshly desires, carrying out the inclinations of our flesh and thoughts, and we were by nature children under wrath as the others were also. But God, who is rich in mercy, because of his great love that he had for us, made us alive with Christ even though we were dead in trespasses. You are saved by grace! (Ephesians 2:1-5)

Dead and alive are about as opposite and vivid

a comparison as Paul could make. Death is a complete separation from life. My depression honestly feels like a separation from my own life. But, I am a Christian. I am no longer dead in my sins, but alive in Christ. No matter how I feel, the truth is that I am alive in Christ.

Since this depression episode is just setting in, I still remember what non-depression feels like. Today I can objectively hold that before me and see the hopelessness, darkness, death, and numbness on one side and the joy, life, color, and hope on the other.

It gives me a clearer picture of the place I really was when I was living without Christ; what my spiritual reality is apart from God, no matter how it felt at the time. It also reminds me of the daily hope, joy, and vibrancy available to me as I am alive in Christ today.

I realize that if you don't struggle with depression, this might not resonate with you. Instead, I'd urge you to think for a few moments about your experience with the reality of death. It seems like I've been surrounded by more of that than usual in the last several months. Compare death to the hope of a new baby. Compare the lifeless look of trees and shrubs in the winter to the re-greening, re-budding, and re-flowering of spring.

It's spring here in Middle Tennessee and life is worth celebrating in all of its forms, particularly when we contrast it with death. But the most important truth to celebrate is that you are alive in Christ. What a beautiful gift!

✤ Spend a few moments contrasting things of death and things of life. What comes to mind?

✤ The truth of being a believer is that you are alive in Christ, no matter how you feel today. How is that truth helpful?

Abba, Daddy,

Thank you for the beautiful gift of life in Christ. Thank you, for no matter how deep in the muck I feel like I'm in, the truth is that I'm alive in you. You're the expert at making dead things alive. Making broken things whole. Give me a fresh experience of that today.

I love you. Amen.

WEEK 05
DAY 04

I've been accused of plagiarism twice. Once legitimately. My freshman year in college, I was in a two-semester philosophy course. It was a small class, with only 12 or 15 students. We met at the professor's home and his wife, who was from South America, would serve us amazing Brazilian sweets and snacks when we took a break. I've never before or since experienced anything quite like that exchange of ideas and cultures.

I was from a very small town in northern Indiana. I had no background in philosophy or European history. We spent the whole year reading philosophers' works and discussing what they meant. It was a time-consuming class—we had to read one or more philosophical works each week. This was not beach reading. It was more like fighting your way through waist-high brambles with a butter knife! In addition, we had to write a three-page paper every week.

The first half of each paper was a summary of the author's philosophy. I had never been exposed to rigorous academic standards, and I got a little sloppy one week. I was summoned to the professor's office and given a stern introduction to the idea of plagiarism—copying someone else's work. I did not do it again. The

professor who gave me a D on my final paper in college disagreed. But she was wrong!

In *Steal Like An Artist*, Austin Kleon says, "What a good artist understands is that nothing comes from nowhere. All creative work builds on what came before. Nothing is completely original."[1]

Unless you're God.

God spins galaxies out of nothing with a word. He knit you together inside your mother's womb. When he spoke, seas formed. Animals came to life. Birds flew. And plants bloomed. His creation is vast and rich, and long after he created it, we're still learning new things every day.

> *Therefore, if anyone is in Christ, he is a new creation; the old has passed away, and see, the new has come!* (2 Corinthians 5:17)

A new creation is not simply you, cleaned up. It's new. It's not a plagiarized, rearranged version of who you are. If you are in Christ, he has made you to be something completely new. You are changed in purpose, in identity, in ownership, in spiritual position. Your past no longer defines you. Your mistakes no longer condemn you. You are changed. You are an utterly new creation.

- What's important to you about the fact that God as Creator has made you into something new?
- If your past or your mistakes no longer identify you, how do you deal with them?

I Am a New Creation

Father,

You are thoroughly amazing. I can't come up with a single new thing, and yet you are a never-ending supply. I'm in awe of your creative nature. Thank you for creating a new me. Help me absorb the truth of that in new ways today.

I love you. Amen.

WEEK 05
DAY 05

When I was growing up, you could call a friend on a landline. If they weren't home, you might be able to leave them a message (if they had an answering machine). If you couldn't leave a message and they didn't live nearby, you'd just have to try later or wait until you saw them next. Talking to someone overseas was an ordeal involving operators and often failed connections.

Now we have phones in our pockets that allow us to talk, text, or video message anyone at any time. Last spring, when I was in Greece, I could text my family and friends, send photos, and talk to them as if we were at my kitchen table.

We have access to a constant stream of news and events on both a local and global level. More than we can absorb. While we are thoroughly digitally connected, it's been argued that we're less and less soul-invested in those connections.

I'm not bashing technology; it's opened up amazing possibilities for us. But I do want you to think about access. As consumers in the online marketplace, the most valuable commodity we own is our email address. Why? Because giving it to me allows me access to your world in a way even snail mail doesn't. It gives me a connected channel to your inbox where I can pursue

a relationship with you. Without that email address, I'm forced to rely on you recognizing my ads, hearing about me from your friends, or searching me out on your own.

Access is a powerful thing. People want to connect with influential people, whether they have political, social, or financial power. Even children recognize this. I read a story recently about Tad Lincoln, the youngest son of President and Mary Todd Lincoln. When his family lived in the White House, he had free run of the Executive Mansion. Because of the privileges of his position and his access to all portions of the mansion, he began acting as a gatekeeper and charging visitors a nickel to meet with his father![2]

In our social media-connected world, it's easier than ever to gain access to people you'd like to meet. But how many powerful people can you access on a 24/7 basis?

We have also obtained access through him by faith into this grace in which we stand, and we rejoice in the hope of the glory of God. (Romans 5:2)

For through him we both have access in one spirit to the Father. (Ephesians 2:18)

In him we have boldness and confident access through faith in him. (Ephesians 3:12)

You have access to the Creator of all things any time you like. Better than VIP backstage passes. Better than living in the White House with a president. Better, because there is never a moment when you don't have access to your Heavenly Father.

He's never too busy. Never too tired. Never too preoccupied. He's never too involved with someone else. There's never anything too big or too small for him to want to hear from you. He's provided that access through Christ's death, resurrection, and the Holy Spirit in you.

He always wants to listen to you

✤ How do you think about your access to God?

✤ Do you take advantage of the access you have? What's your pattern of communication with him?

✤ What does your access say about your identity?

Abba, Daddy,

When I really stop to consider who you are and that I have your ear absolutely whenever I want, I'm filled with awe and shyness—or something like shyness. But your Word says that I should have boldness and confidence in my access to you. You want to hear from me! Thank you so much for that. So often people are too busy or too important, but you never are. Thank you for lavishing me with time, attention, and love. Thank you for the access I have as your beloved child.

I love you. Amen.

WEEK 05
DAY 06

When Jerry Maguire, played by Tom Cruise, emotionally told his secretary, Renee Zellweger, "I love you. You complete me," in the 1996 movie, Jerry Maguire, it brought into the modern culture an idea as old as Plato. We spend an extraordinary amount of time looking for completeness. Looking for someone else who can fill the places we feel are empty. Looking for someone who will complete us.

In his Symposium, Plato gave Aristophanes an argument to present that humans were originally both male and female until Zeus, concerned that they were too powerful, split them in two, creating two halves of a whole, destined forever to be searching for their other half. Ryan Christensen of Brigham Young University says, "Within the play, Plato objects to Aristophanes' account of the origin of the genders and the idea that one person can be half of a whole. 'According to Plato, you can't truly love something, whether half or whole, unless it is truly good. You can never be satisfied with something that is less than perfection.'"[3]

Obviously, Aristophanes' argument gained traction as some form of it is still with us today, both in Tom Cruise movies and in each of our lives. We look to a lot of things to complete

us. We cling to other people, to achievement, to status, and to possessions. We constantly seek after newer, bigger, brighter things. After more sensation or less sensation. We're always yearning for things we don't have and envious of people who have them. We're continually told by media that we're not pretty enough, skinny enough, wealthy enough, or smart enough. We're kept dissatisfied and discontent.

But you already have everything within you that you need to be whole. You don't need a soul mate to complete you. You don't need a new job or a new body. You have everything you need for life right now.

> *His divine power has given us everything required for life and godliness through the knowledge of him who called us by his own glory and goodness.* (2 Peter 1:3)

We often live with a sense that something is missing. That there's more. And we're right: there is. There's always more of God available to us.

> *So you also are complete through your union with Christ, who is the head over every ruler and authority.* (Colossians 2:10 NLT)

If you are a Christ-follower, you have everything you need right now in Christ. You are complete in him.

- What do you seek to fulfill that sense of needing more in your life?

I Am Complete in Christ

✤ What are some ways you can think of that Christ completes you?

✤ What parts of your life tend to breed discontent and dissatisfaction?

✤ How could your relationship with Christ eliminate it?

Jesus,

You complete me. Not my partner, friends, family, weight, career, children, or ministry. You. You provide all I need for life and godliness. Help me understand that truth in a very real way today. Help me live out, in practical ways, the reality of it.

I love you. Amen.

WEEK 05
DAY 07

This week, we've looked at what God says it means for us to be "in Christ." Do you have a better understanding of your privilege and position in Christ? We discovered who we are in Christ, that we are alive in Christ, that we are a new creation, connected and complete in Christ.

What has God spoken to your heart this week?

How have these truths changed the way you think or feel about yourself?

Father,

"In Christ" seems so foreign to my everyday reality. It seems something more like fantasy, but that's not true. It's real and crucial for me to understand. Help open my heart to accepting and believing my true position in Christ. My true identity in him.

I love you. Amen.

Next week, we'll look at the spiritual results of our identity in Christ. What does God say about our spiritual self?

WHAT IS MY SPIRITUAL IDENTITY?

WEEK 06

WEEK 06
DAY 01

Daily life usually seems more real to us than our spiritual life, but it's not. This week we're going to look at some of the important spiritual realities and how they affect our identity. We'll cover:

✤ I am blameless in God's sight.

✤ I am spiritually blessed.

✤ I am in a spiritual battle.

✤ I am clothed in Christ.

✤ I am sealed by God.

PRAY

Father,

It's hard sometimes to remember that spiritual realities are just as real as physical ones. This week, as I read about the spiritual truths that are part of my identity, would you make them very real to me? Help me absorb them into how I see myself. Align my perspective with yours.

Thank you for all you do and all the countless ways you've provided for me. You are vast beyond my ability to understand and yet within me. Thank you for wanting me to know who I am.

I love you. Amen.

MEDITATION VERSE

Think about this verse throughout the week. Write it on a sticky note and leave it where you'll see it often. Or, go to **www.whogodsaysyouare.link/resources** and download the pdf with the weekly meditation verses. Print and hang the appropriate verse for each week where you'll see it often. Found in the same online resource list, you'll find a guide for meditating on scripture that will explain what it means to meditate on scripture, what it doesn't mean and offer suggestions.

*F*OR HE CHOSE US
IN HIM
BEFORE THE FOUNDATION
OF THE WORLD,
TO BE HOLY
AND BLAMELESS
IN LOVE
BEFORE HIM.

EPH 1: 4

WEEK 06
DAY 02

One summer when I was growing up, there was an incident involving my sister's teeth.

My brother chased my sister around the yard. I don't remember why, but she probably deserved being chased. He chased her around the house, out to the end of the pier and back into the house. She ran upstairs, into her room, and threw herself on her bed. Our house had radiant heat with tall iron radiators in each room.

When she hit the bed at high speed, her mouth collided with the radiator at the head of her bed. Her perfectly straight front teeth lost the battle in the impact, breaking in half.

My mother was not pleased. Not even a little bit. She'd like me to add that this was not an isolated game they were playing; it was the most recent battle in a summer-long war the two had engaged in. As a result of this skirmish and the destruction of the only teeth in the house not requiring orthodontics, my brother and sister spent much of the summer scraping the paint off the pier and repainting it.

Where was I? I was completely uninvolved. As far as this particular episode goes, I was totally blameless. And, boy, did that feel good! I was the golden child for a brief and shining month while they were in the doghouse.

I Am Blameless in God's Sight

Why did that feel so good? Because there's so much I can legitimately be blamed for that weighs me down. We try to avoid it. We do everything we can to shift blame to others. Do you remember what Adam said when God confronted him about eating from the forbidden tree? He shifted the blame to Eve. And what did Eve do? Shifted the blame to the snake. We're experts at that particular maneuver.

But when we come face to face with the One who can see through any attempt on our part to escape or shift blame, when we're faced with the One so powerful that any posturing on our part is utterly ridiculous, when we're faced with the One who knows ALL OF IT—every minute motivation, desire, and detail—we are, should be, or will be crushed by the weight of our guilt.

We have so much to be blamed for.

Blessed is the God and Father of our Lord Jesus Christ, who has blessed us with every spiritual blessing in the heavens in Christ. For he chose us in him, before the foundation of the world, to be holy and blameless in love before him. (Ephesians 1:3-4)

And yet, instead of that crushing blame, there are no fingers pointing. There are no accusations. There is no shame. In Christ, you are blameless before God.

Stunningly, beautifully, amazingly blameless.

Sit for a moment and think of the things that you should be blamed for. For some of you that

may be a well-rehearsed list. Imagine it as dirt that you can't brush off. How many layers cover you? How filthy are you?

No matter how much we posture and pose in this life, the truth is that spiritually, we look like Charlie Brown's friend, Pigpen. And yet, because of Christ's death and resurrection, you are blameless before God. No accusation. No penalty. No shame. Blameless.

Consider for a few moments that everything you can think of, all those reasons you could be blamed you thought of a moment ago. They are all covered by Christ's sacrifice. Yes, even the huge ones. Even the smallest ones. Even the intentional ones. All of them. Covered by Christ. Let yourself feel the impact, beauty, and freedom of that. You are blameless in his sight.

Father,

I'm pretty sure if I really understood the depth of my sin against you, I'd be crushed by the weight of it. I'm so grateful for your love for me. So grateful you've made a way for me to be blameless in your sight. Help me stand in that truth and act accordingly.

I love you. Amen.

WEEK 06
DAY 02

"God bless you!" or "Bless you!" is a response to a sneeze.

"Bless my stars!" is an expression of surprise. "Bless my stars, Bubba passed all his classes last quarter!"

"Bless my lucky stars!" expresses an appreciation for a beneficial event or occurrence. "Bless my lucky stars! Aunt Betty just brought me a pecan pie for no reason!"

"Bless your heart" everywhere except the South is an expression of fondness, appreciation for someone, or concern.

"Bless your heart" in the South can mean something slightly different depending on the tone, volume, and how much sass it's delivered with. It typically sounds like front-porch sweet tea, but is most often intended as a patronizing comment about someone's lack of brain cells (or other intended insult).

For example, "Emma Sue just couldn't seem to squeeze her thighs into those shorts today, could she, now? She's spillin' out all over the map. Bless her heart!" The phrase softens the blow of an insult, making it appropriate for polite conversation. It's also typically delivered with a (fake or vicious) smile and syrupy sweetness. I'm not suggesting you say something like that, but if

you visit the South for any length of time, you'll hear it.

A few less common idioms,

"Bless your pointy little head!" is a condescending phrase slightly more straightforward and obvious than "Bless your heart!"[1]

"Bless the world with his heels" means to be hanged.[2] As in, "Bubba blessed the world with his heels this mornin' and his mama, Emma Sue's so sad. He killed his cousin with his own pickup truck in front of the police station, bless his heart!"

And heard in the UK and Australia,

"Bless her cotton socks!" is an expression of fondness or appreciation.[3] "My son just took Emma Sue a bouquet of tulips to ease her heart, bless his cotton socks!"

"I'm so blessed" appears on social media frequently. It often precedes a paragraph listing the wonderful accomplishments of the person speaking or that of their family. Also known as a "humble brag."

We toss the word "bless" around freely. We use it so casually that when we read it in scripture, we tend to skim over it without thinking.

Blessed is the God and Father of our Lord Jesus Christ, who has blessed us with every spiritual blessing in the heavens in Christ.
(Ephesians 1:3)

God blesses us with every spiritual blessing. More amazing than Bubba's passing grades, more important than being blessed with a pecan pie, and more genuine than a Southerner's "Bless your heart." According to Kathy Howard, God's

blessings are "spiritual in nature and eternal in scope. The blessings He lavishes on us are exactly what we need to deepen our relationship with God, grow to Christ-likeness, and fulfill God's purposes for our lives."[4]

GotQuestions.org says, "The word blessing in Ephesians 1:3 is a translation of the Greek word eulogy, and it means 'to speak well of.' Since God is the one acting in this verse, we can say that God has spoken good things about us, or pronounced good things for our benefit."[5]

As you continue to read the first chapter in Ephesians, you'll find a handful of those blessings listed, as Paul pours them out in a 202-word sentence (in the Greek). They include being chosen to be holy and blameless before him, adoption, redemption, forgiveness of sins, an inheritance, and the Holy Spirit. Many of the "I Am" identity statements in this book fall into this category of spiritual blessing.

You've been given spiritual gifts and realities beyond measure. Don't let the casual or idiomatic way we use the word "bless" keep you from appreciating the deep significance of what it means for you.

You are spiritually blessed.

To use one more culturally appropriated idiom in a truly serious way, spend some time counting your spiritual blessings today. Think through the blessings listed in Ephesians and the "I Ams" that we've studied in the last several weeks and consider how blessed you really are and where you would be without them.

I Am Spiritually Blessed

Father,

I'm so grateful for you blessing me in such rich, generous, eternal ways. Especially today, thank you for...(insert those that have really struck you today).

I love you. Amen.

WEEK 06
DAY 04

I've lived in the South now for more than ten years. Like most people in the Nashville area, I'm a transplant. I moved to Tennessee during the summer, and by the time I went home for Thanksgiving that year, I had snuggled into my new ZIP Code like I did into the heavy coat I had to run out and buy for Thanksgiving in the North. I told my family, "You realize you don't have to live like this, right?" It doesn't take long for this land of beautiful green hills and steamy summers to seduce you.

Rick Bragg is a Pulitzer Prize-winning journalist and writer. He has said about the South:

> I know I grew up in the time when a young man in a baggy suit and slicked-down hair stood spraddle-legged in the crossroads of history and talked hot and mean about the colored, giving my poor and desperate people a reason to feel superior to somebody, to anybody. I know that even as the words of George Wallace rang through my Alabama, the black family who lived down the dirt road from our house sent fresh-picked corn and other food to the poor white lady and her three sons, because they knew their

daddy had run off, because hungry does not have a color.[6]

I wonder if, north of here, they might even run out of stories someday. It may seem silly, but it is cold up there, too cold to mosey, to piddle, to loafer, and summer only lasts a week and a half. The people spit the words out so fast when they talk, like they are trying to discard them somehow, banish them, rather than relish the sound and the story. We will not run out of them here. We talk like we are tasting something.[7]

Rick Bragg captures the heartbeat of the South in vivid detail in his books, articles, and column for Southern Living magazine. His language is full of the rhythms and cadence of his beloved region. He writes of the beauty, the darkness, the poverty, and the joy of growing up in rural Alabama. His Southern-ness saturates his writing. His location is inseparable from his identity.

Where you are is an important part of your identity as well. What seems real is grocery shopping, TV watching, facebook scrolling, and parenting. What is just as real is that you're in the midst of a spiritual battle.

For our struggle is not against flesh and blood, but against the rulers, against the authorities, against the cosmic powers of this darkness, against evil, spiritual forces in the heavens. (Ephesians 6:12)

For although we live in the flesh, we do not wage war according to the flesh, since the weapons of our warfare are not of the

flesh, but are powerful through God for the demolition of strongholds. We demolish arguments and every proud thing that is raised up against the knowledge of God, and we take every thought captive to obey Christ. (2 Corinthians 10:3-5)

In an interview published by the Billy Graham Evangelistic Association, Tony Evans, a speaker, writer, pastor, and Bible teacher, said, "We are suffering from a Greek philosophical orientation to life, all the way back to Plato, who separated the spiritual and the physical world. He kept them in two different compartments. Under the lordship of Jesus Christ, the secular becomes sanctified. It is now spiritual because we invite God to be in every situation."[8]

Our struggles are spiritual ones.

You do have to go to the grocery store and parent your children (TV and Facebook are optional). The realities of life described by authors like Rick Bragg touch us, because we've experienced what they describe. But, they're only a part of the picture. The spiritual realm is just as real, just as important, and arguably more powerful than the parts of life you can see, hear, and touch.

꙳ How should you respond to the understanding that you're in the midst of an ongoing spiritual battle?

꙳ How does it change your perspective on who you are?

Father,

*My physical reality seems so much more real
than the spiritual one. Help me understand
the truth of my spiritual reality. Help me live
as if the spiritual battle is real—because it is.
Help me know what changes I need to make in
my life because of that and help me trust your
description of me more than my own senses.*

I love you, Amen.

WEEK 06
DAY 05

The clothes you wear say a lot about who you are. I've been in online groups where women say that they habitually and intentionally wore drab, shapeless clothes in order to hide.

We use clothing to proclaim ourselves affiliated with a particular brand. Do you own a shirt with a brand logo, tagline, or message? Odds are pretty good the answer is "Yes."

The styles we wear can also indicate a lifestyle or activity we identify with. Skateboarders dress differently than hunters, who dress differently than debutantes.

We use style, logos, or brands to show status or prosperity. What does a Gucci handbag or a Rolex watch indicate? This isn't a modern phenomenon. Scottish clans have been identified by their clothing for centuries.

In biblical times, the color purple was an indication of wealth and prosperity. Nelson's New Illustrated Bible Dictionary says that purple dye was harvested from a gland in a mollusk and piles of the discarded shells can still be found in Tyre and Sidon. It took a lot of manpower to extract the dye, and it took 250,000 mollusks to make a single ounce of it! Do you begin to understand why purple garments and decoration were a sign of wealth and position?

I Am Clothed in Christ

What you wear says something about you.

For those of you who were baptized into Christ have been clothed with Christ. (Galatians 3:27)

I rejoice greatly in the Lord,
I exult in my God;
for he has clothed me with the garments of salvation
and wrapped me in a robe of righteousness,
as a groom wears a turban
and as a bride adorns herself with her jewels.
(Isaiah 61:10)

We are clothed with Christ, with salvation and righteousness. This says everything about us to God. He does not see our sinfulness when he looks at us, but instead, he sees Christ's perfection.

But it also says something about us in our world. Or, it should.

✤ You are clothed with Christ—this is a fact, not a decision you make, like getting dressed in the morning. How visible is this garment to the world?

✤ What in your attitude, behavior, words, or actions would make this spiritual clothing more visible in your world?

Father,

Thank you so very much for giving me clothing more lasting, more precious, and more beautiful than anything made on earth. Thank you for wrapping me up in Christ in a way that cannot be worn out, torn, or misplaced. Help me to consciously allow this garment to be my identity. Help me remember each morning as I get dressed that my spiritual clothing matters more.

I love you. Amen.

WEEK 06
DAY 06

"I'm going to go look for something in my room. I'll come right back and start the laundry, Mom," says my 12-year-old. I now have a few options. Let him disappear into the abyss of his room and conveniently "forget" the laundry that needs to be done. Or, "Okay, honey, hand me your phone and I'll leave it right here on this laundry pile until you get back."

Now, my son could easily pick up a phone from a pile of laundry and still forget that he was supposed to put the laundry in the washer, but you get the idea. His phone is valuable enough to him that Mom can use it as a guarantee that he'll return to reclaim it.

In him you also were sealed with the promised Holy Spirit when you heard the word of truth, the gospel of your salvation, and when you believed. The Holy Spirit is the down payment of our inheritance, until the redemption of the possession, to the praise of his glory. (Ephesians 1:13-14)

Let's play reporter, shall we? I was a journalism major for a time in my college years. The basics of reporting are the five W's and an H. These are also the basics of birthday party invitation

issuing and as a parent, I believe they are woefully underutilized. But, that's way off topic!

Who? God.

What? Sealed you as a guarantee of your inheritance.

Why? For the praise of his glory.

When? At the time you believed the gospel.

Where? In Christ.

How? With himself, with the Holy Spirit.

There's always a chance that my pre-teen boy would get distracted by a TV, laptop, or food and not return to get his phone. But God gives us himself as a guarantee. Is there anything he could have done to give you more assurance? He gave Christ to overcome our sin and the Holy Spirit to guarantee the fulfillment of Christ's sacrifice for you. John Piper says,

> God's great desire for his people is that we feel secure in his love and in his power...Since God does all things for the praise of his glory, and since believing his Word magnifies that glory, therefore God takes decisive steps to secure for himself the magnification of his glory forever: he seals the believer with the Holy Spirit, and guarantees that we will come to our inheritance praising his glory. God is so passionately committed to having a people for his own possession who live forever for the praise of his glory that he is not about to let our eternal destiny depend on our native powers of willing or doing. He commissions his Holy Spirit to enter our lives and to make us secure forever.[9]

I Am Sealed by God

✽ How does this affect your identity?

✽ What does this do for your confidence?

Father,

You chose me before the foundations of the world to be set apart for your purposes and blameless before you, and you've made the way for that to happen. I'm so thankful. You've given me the Holy Spirit. You've given of yourself in such astonishing ways. Thank you for that gift. Thank you for leaving such assurance that I am yours. Thank you for leaving such assurance that you love me. Thank you for leaving such assurance that you will follow through on every one of your promises.

I love you. Amen.

WEEK 06
DAY 07

This week, we've looked at what God says about the spiritual realities of being a Christ-follower. We learned we are blameless in his sight, blessed, in a spiritual battle, clothed in Christ, and sealed by God.

What has God spoken to your heart this week?

How have these truths changed the way you think or feel about yourself?

Father,

Spiritual blessings sometimes don't seem as real or as practical as if you blessed me in physical, tangible ways. But they're far more important. Help me truly believe that. Help me seek spiritual blessings over physical ones. Help me value spiritual truths and hunger for more.

I love you. Amen.

Next week we'll look at different ways God describes us. Have you ever called yourself a jewel?

HOW DOES GOD DESCRIBE ME?

WEEK 07

WEEK 07
DAY 01

Have you ever listened to a friend or loved one introduce you to someone new? You hear what they find important and interesting about you. You hear what they value in you. You hopefully hear things that surprise and delight you! This week we're going to listen in as God describes us. We'll look at the following statements you can make:

❖ I am a vessel.

❖ I am a jewel.

❖ I am a new creation.

❖ I am a temple.

❖ I am a living stone.

PRAY

Father,

Open my heart this week to the truths you have for me. Help me understand your Word and apply it to my life. Give me the insights you want me to learn and absorb. Mold my perception of myself to be in line with your Word.

I love you. Amen.

MEDITATION VERSE

Think about this verse throughout the week. Write it on a sticky note and leave it where you'll see it often. Or, go to **www. whogodsaysyouare. link/resources** and download the pdf with the weekly meditation verses. Print and hang the appropriate verse for each week where you'll see it often. Found in the same online resource list, you'll find a guide for meditating on scripture that will explain what it means to meditate on scripture, what it doesn't mean and offer suggestions.

DON'T YOU YOURSELVES
K N O W
THAT YOU ARE GOD'S
T E M P L E
AND THAT THE SPIRIT
O F   G O D
LIVES
IN
Y O U ?

1 COR 3:16

WEEK 07
DAY 01

I love rocks. Not enough to be a real rock hound, so maybe I should say instead that I like rocks a lot. I tend to pick them up wherever I'm visiting. I'd love to say I have a beautiful collection from all the places I've been, but that would require more organization and follow-through than this artist-brained girl seems to have.

My son enjoys them, too. One of his favorite things to do as a youngster was to take a big hammer and break open geodes. Geodes look like ordinary rocks from the outside. Standard-issue rocks that are usually grayish or brownish, but definitely bland-ish. Inside, however, they have a cavity lined with crystals or other minerals. When you break them open, they're unique and beautiful on the inside. A beautiful interior is tucked away inside these ordinary-looking rocks.

I had a geode experience this morning walking into my eye doctor's office. They've built a new building and moved in last week, just in time for my annual appointment. The outside is nice, but nothing particularly special. The inside, however, is stunning. They weren't able to save a historic home on the property, so they salvaged every possible scrap and used it on the inside of the

new building. The interior is a surprise when you come through the front doors for the first time. It's an airy, expansive room full of weathered brick, old fireplace mantles, original fixtures, and a modern aesthetic. The exterior really doesn't give a hint that there's a special beauty inside.

> *Now in a large house there are not only gold and silver vessels, but also those of wood and clay; some for honorable use and some for dishonorable. So if anyone purifies himself from anything dishonorable, he will be a special instrument, set apart, useful to the Master, prepared for every good work.* (2 Timothy 2:20-21)

A vessel is a container, and Paul calls us vessels. Like geodes, and one particular eye doctor's office, we might be ordinary-seeming, but we carry within us something far more beautiful and valuable than crystals, or vintage decor. We hold the very Spirit of God.

> *You, however, are not in the flesh, but in the Spirit, if indeed the Spirit of God lives in you. If anyone does not have the Spirit of Christ, he does not belong to him. Now if Christ is in you, the body is dead because of sin, but the Spirit gives life because of righteousness. And if the Spirit of him who raised Jesus from the dead lives in you, then he who raised Christ from the dead will also bring your mortal bodies to life through his Spirit who lives in you.* (Romans 8:9-11)

> *Now we have this treasure in clay jars, so that this extraordinary power may be from God and not from us.* (2 Corinthians 4:7)

I Am a Vessel

Amazing when you think about it. Your body carries around the living God who created the universe! Our bodies, while intricate, fascinating, and amazing in themselves are still ordinary when compared to our Creator God. They're breakable, fallible, and temporary.

God is not outside of us as a long-distance relationship, but as close as your own heart and lungs. Closer than any other person you have a relationship with.

🌼 What does being a vessel holding the God who created the universe mean to you?

🌼 What impact does having this treasure in jars of clay have for the kingdom?

🌼 What kinds of actions or attitudes does it inspire in you?

Father,

You are what is beautiful inside of me. Thank you for making this ordinary vessel something extraordinary. Help me behave and treat my body in honorable ways, as it is your home. Help me to pursue righteous living, faithfulness, love, kindness, patience, and peace. Draw my heart to you in ever deeper ways.

I love you. Amen.

WEEK 07
DAY 03

I love jewelry. I'm not sure why, but I love the variety, the artistry, and the beauty of it. I love diamonds and all other gems, but not because of their value; I love them because of their beauty and uniqueness. But, they certainly can be valuable. In 2017, the average diamond engagement ring in the United States had a 1.2-carat center stone and cost over $6,300.[1] Gemstones are called "precious stones" and wealthy and powerful people have always adorned themselves with valuable jewels.

The largest gem-quality diamond ever found was discovered in South Africa in January of 1905. The Cullinan, as it was named, was given to King Edward VII of the United Kingdom as a 66th birthday gift in 1907. After a few months of study (It was a difficult diamond to cut.), it was divided into nine major stones, 96 smaller stones, and about 19.5 carats of unpolished diamonds.[2]

The two largest stones are known as the Star of Africa and the Lesser Star of Africa and are on display in the Tower of London as part of the Crown Jewels of the United Kingdom. These, along with the other nine major stones have adorned British royalty since the early 1900s.[3] Cullinan I, or the Star of Africa, is about 530 carats and a little over 2-1/4" in length and is

currently the largest clear-colored, cut diamond in the world.[4] This is more than 500 times the size of the average American engagement ring diamond. The total value of the gems that once made up the Cullinan diamond is estimated in the billions of dollars.[5]

By any type of evaluation, these royal stones are valuable. Precious gemstones. A treasured possession of the Royal Family. They wear them. Protect them. And insure them for vast sums of money! The one-carat engagement rings are also treasured possessions of their owners.

At that time those who feared the Lord spoke to one another. The Lord took notice and listened. So a book of remembrance was written before him for those who feared the Lord and had high regard for his name. "They will be mine," says the Lord of Armies, "my own possession on the day I am preparing. I will have compassion on them as a man has compassion on his son who serves him." (Malachi 3:16-17)

Other Bible versions translate "my own possession" as:
KJV: my jewels
NIV and ESV: my treasured possession
NLT: my own special treasure
You are infinitely more valuable than the Cullinan diamonds. You are God's treasured possession. His jewel.

Malachi was writing to a generation much like ours; belief in God and personal righteousness was out of fashion. Religious skepticism was the prevailing cultural attitude. In the midst of that, God tells "those that feared the Lord"

that he hears them. He listens. And a book of remembrance has been written for them.

A book of remembrance was kept by kings to reward those who acted on his behalf or were due to receive a reward for service. Rewards weren't always issued at the time of service, but the book meant that the debt wouldn't be forgotten. God doesn't need a book to remember, but this verse was an assurance to his people that they were seen, they were heard, and they were not forgotten.

You are precious to him. He hasn't forgotten you. He hears and listens.

✤ God describes you as a treasured possession, a jewel. How does this line up with how you see yourself?

✤ How does this analogy (that of a jewel or treasure) affect your understanding about who you are?

Father,

I often see myself as flawed, as not valuable. Help me understand who I am based on your perspective and truth, not mine. Help me see myself as your treasured possession. As a jewel. Draw me toward your heart. May I be one who fears the Lord in all of my beliefs, actions, and attitudes. Help me remember that you see me,

I Am a Jewel

hear me, and care for me at all times. Let me see my value as one given by the Lord of the universe.

I love you. Amen.

WEEK 07
DAY 04

Therefore, if anyone is in Christ, he is a new creation; the old has passed away, and see, the new has come! (2 Corinthians 5:17)

This is a popular memory verse and one that's often sloganized and printed on mugs. Many years ago, I was given a notepad with this verse and a cute illustration on each sheet of paper. Knowing the state of my closets and love for illustration, I probably still have it somewhere. It had cartoonish elephants flying around on colorful, whimsical little wings. First of all, those wings couldn't possibly hold an elephant in the air, and second, that's not something that could ever happen, no matter how hard you try to breed whimsically-shaped birds with elephants. But that was the point.

When you believe in Christ, you become something brand new.

Something not possible without Christ.

Recently, my father brought me a book with a chapter discussing our identity. *Classic Christianity, Life's Too Short To Miss The Real Thing*, by Bob George, is a book my brother gave my dad many years ago when he was about to step into a relationship with Christ. When talking about our identity, Mr. George shares a common

analogy: Who we are changes when we believe in Christ like a caterpillar changes into a butterfly. The butterfly is a new creation. There's a good chance you've heard that before. But he said something further that has changed the way I think about being a new creation. He says:

If you were to see a butterfly, it would never occur to you to say, "Hey everybody! Come look at this good-looking converted worm!" Why not? After all, it was a worm. And it was "converted." No, now it is a new creature, and you don't think of it in terms of what it was. You see it as it is now—a butterfly.

In exactly the same way, God sees you as His new creature in Christ. Although you might not always act like a good butterfly— you might land on things you shouldn't, or forget you are a butterfly and crawl around with your old worm buddies—the truth of the matter is, you are never going to be a worm again!

This is why the usual New Testament word for a person in Christ is, "saint," meaning "holy one." Paul, for example, in nearly all his letters addressed them to the "saints." Yet all the time I hear Christians refer to themselves as "just an old sinner saved by grace." No! That's like calling a butterfly a converted worm. We were sinners and we were saved by grace, but the Word of God calls us saints from the moment we become identified with Christ.

Some people ask, "But, I still commit sins. Doesn't that make me a sinner?"

I answer, "It depends on whether your

identity is determined by your behavior—
what you do—or by who you are in God's
eyes."

✤ How do you choose to determine your
identity? As the world does, by your
behavior? Or, as God does, by your identity in
Christ? Obviously, this is the whole question
we're working on in this study, but it's good
to take stock as we're about halfway through.
Has your perception of your identity shifted?

✤ Have you ever called yourself "a sinner
saved by grace"? Do you need to change
that description? (She says, scurrying off to
change her website bio!)

✤ You are a new creation; the old has passed
away. What has passed away? How are you a
new creation?

Father,

*Your work constantly astounds me! You've
turned me into something new; something
not possible before. You've cleansed me from
all unrighteousness and clothed me in Christ.
Thank you. Thank you for giving me the
perspective today of seeing myself as you do,
flying with the butterflies (or elephants). Help
me act in ways that align with my new identity.
Help me understand that I am a new creature
and leave behind the ways, speech, attitudes,
habits, behaviors, and loves of the old.*

I love you. Amen.

WEEK 07
DAY 05

When David became king of a united Israel, he realized that he was living in splendor and God's dwelling place on earth was a tent. He wanted to build God a temple. But God, said, "No," and gave that task to Solomon, David's son. Instead, David began preparing for the temple. He began to lay aside money and provisions. Later, Solomon built an incredible temple. The cedar wood walls were carved and overlaid with gold. Two tall gold-covered statues of cherubim with fifteen-foot wingspans stood in the inner sanctuary. The temple was magnificent.

It was the place where God's Spirit dwelt on earth. It was where God's people came to meet with him, learn about him, and honor him; the place where sacrifices were made for the sins of the nation and its people.

But, as we tend to do, in time, God's people turned from him, and he allowed the temple to be destroyed. It was rebuilt under the direction of Nehemiah, and as Jerusalem was repopulated, worship and sacrifices were reinstated. This brings us to the New Testament.

Jesus answered, "Destroy this temple, and I will raise it up in three days."

Therefore the Jews said, "This temple took forty-six years to build, and will you raise it up in three days?"
But he was speaking about the temple of his body. So when he was raised from the dead, his disciples remembered that he had said this, and they believed the Scripture and the statement Jesus had made. (John 2:19-22)

Jesus becomes the ultimate place where sinners meet with God, the temple of our times. A single sacrifice for all sins. The threads of the Old Testament covenant come together within him.

Dr. Don Carson said, "He is the ultimate priest. He is the ultimate sacrifice. His flesh is the veil, and his shattered, broken body is the shattered, broken temple that rises on the third day to become the real meeting place between God and sinful people."[6]

Paul also uses this language about us, about you and me.

Don't you yourselves know that you are God's temple and that the Spirit of God lives in you? (1 Corinthians 3:16)

Don't you know that your body is a temple of the Holy Spirit who is in you, whom you have from God? You are not your own, for you were bought at a price. So glorify God with your body. (1 Corinthians 6:19-20)

As the physical temple in Jerusalem was a dwelling place for God, so are you. The very Spirit of God resides within you. What you do with your body matters. How you treat it matters.

I Am a Temple

✤ How does the truth that you are a temple, a dwelling place of God, change your perception of who you are?

✤ How could we (in general) glorify God with our bodies?

✤ How does it affect how you are treating or using your body? Be specific

Father,

Tracing the temple terminology throughout the whole of scripture is a fascinating study (I only touched on a bit of it here.). The way you've woven threads together throughout history is awe-inspiring. The privilege that I have as a dwelling place for your Spirit is humbling. Thank you for providing the sacrifice for sins in Christ to make that possible, because without the help of the Holy Spirit, I'm lost. Help the understanding of this truth affect my behavior, my attitude toward my body, what I do with it, and how I treat it.

I love you. Amen.

WEEK 07
DAY 06

The Great Chicago Fire burned from Sunday, October 8, until Tuesday, October 10, 1871. It began in a period of drought and spread quickly across the city. The firefighters, likely tired from fighting several fires the week before, responded quickly—but were sent to the wrong address. A variety of other mistakes and miscalls allowed the blaze to rapidly grow out of control.[7]

It jumped the river twice and created a meteorological phenomenon known as a fire whirl.[8] A fire whirl happens in this way: "As overheated air rises, it comes into contact with cooler air and begins to spin creating a tornado-like effect. These fire whirls are likely what drove flaming debris so high and so far."[9] After the fire finally burned itself out and the rain came, the extent of the damage couldn't be determined for days because the remains were so hot.[10]

The fire burned more than 2,000 acres, destroyed more than three square miles of the city, left more than 100,000 residents homeless, and is estimated to have killed about 300 people.[11] Seven buildings survived the fire. Not without damage, but seven buildings withstood the blaze. A few cottages on the north side (how that's even possible, I can't imagine) and a

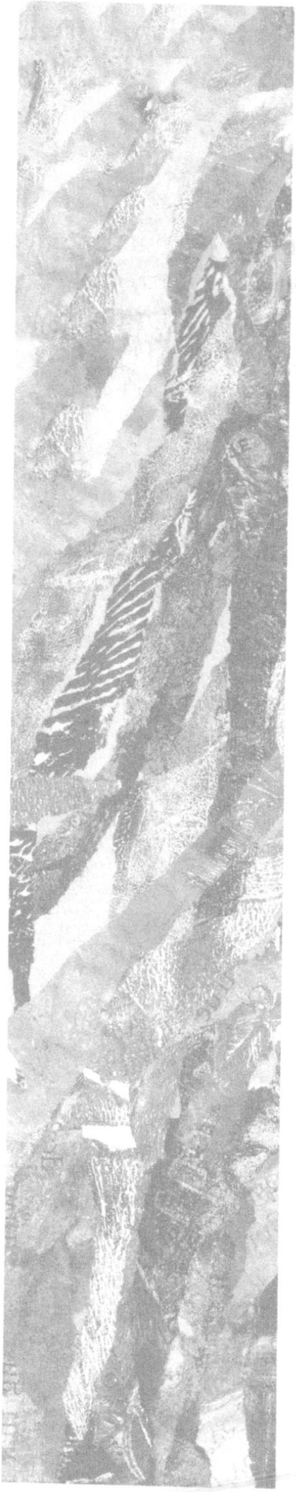

handful of other buildings.[12]

What did the other buildings have in common? Stone or brick construction. Before the fire, Chicago was built of wood. Virtually all of the buildings were wood, many of the roads were wood, and even all the sidewalks were wood. The civic buildings and churches that survived were built of brick or stone.[13]

> *As you come to him, a living stone—rejected by people but chosen and honored by God—you yourselves, as living stones, a spiritual house, are being built to be a holy priesthood to offer spiritual sacrifices acceptable to God through Jesus Christ.* (1 Peter 2:4-5)

I was walking the other day, thinking about the concept of a living stone (a really odd idea, a strange juxtaposition of words) and asking God what he wanted me to focus on in this verse. This is what I heard, "Everything that is permanent, durable, and will stand the test of time and fire in your life, will be built on the foundation cornerstone of my son, Jesus. And whatever you build that way, I promise you, will last."

- Make a list of all the things you're building in your life. Think about all the ways you're investing your time.
- Now, review that list. How many items are built on the cornerstone of Christ? What in your life will last?

I Am A Living Stone

Father,

Help me see clearly my life and pursuits through spiritual eyes. Help me build my heart, my life, my work, my home, and all of my efforts on the cornerstone of Christ. Help me see where that's not happening and help me make the changes you want me to make in my life.

I love you. Amen.

WEEK 07
DAY 07

This week, we've looked at ways that God describes you. We learned that he calls you a vessel, a precious jewel, a new creation, a temple, and a living stone.

What has God spoken to your heart this week?

How have these truths changed the way you think or feel about yourself?

Father,

The things you compare me to are valuable, rare, honoring, and amazing. Help me believe them. Help me be sensitive to the things you want to tell me about myself. Help me learn to think of myself the way you describe me.

I love you. Amen.

Next week we'll look at your spiritual citizenship. Did you know that you hold a dual citizenship?

WHAT IS SPIRITUAL CITIZENSHIP & WHY SHOULD I CARE?

WEEK 08

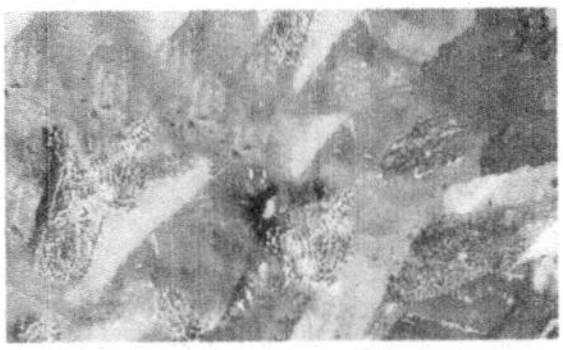

WEEK 08
DAY 01

Where you're born affects the trajectory of your life in some very profound ways. I wasn't born in a slum on the outskirts of Mexico City. I wasn't born in a jungle on the Island of Borneo. I wasn't born in a small town in Northern Finland. If I had been, my perception of the world, my health, my expected life span, my comfort, and my economic status would probably all be very different. I was born in the Midwestern United States in a rural resort community. It's shaped who I am and what I do in life.

My citizenship in the United States brings with it privileges, responsibilities, and rights that would be different if my citizenship was in another nation. We have a physical citizenship, but we have a spiritual one as well. This week, we'll look at what that means. We'll cover:

- I am a citizen of heaven.
- I am a coheir with Christ.
- I am seated at the right hand of God.
- I am an enemy of Satan.
- I have authority over Satan.

PRAY

Father,

As I work through the verses and readings to come, help me understand what my spiritual citizenship means. Help me see the practical implications of this spiritual reality. Spirit, enlighten and encourage me with these passages. I look forward to what you have for me.

I love you. Amen.

MEDITATION VERSE

Think about this verse throughout the week. Write it on a sticky note and leave it where you'll see it often. Or, go to **www.whogodsaysyouare.link/resources** and download the pdf with the weekly meditation verses. Print and hang the appropriate verse for each week where you'll see it often. Found in the same online resource list, you'll find a guide for meditating on scripture that will explain what it means to meditate on scripture, what it doesn't mean and offer suggestions.

IF YOU HAVE BEEN RAISED WITH CHRIST, SEEK THE THINGS ABOVE, WHERE CHRIST IS SEATED AT THE RIGHT HAND OF God
COL 3:1

WEEK 08
DAY 02

When my sister graduated from college and got married, she and her husband moved to Nashville, Tennessee. At that time, I lived in my hometown, not far from my parents, and nine hours away from Nashville. I spent about three long weekends a year with her and came to love the Middle Tennessee area. We would often say as I was leaving how great it would be to live closer to one another.

On one visit—shortly after finding out that my sister and I were both pregnant with boys due less than two months apart—we were talking about wishing our boys could grow up as best friends and not as we-see-each-other-a-few-times-a-year-if-we're-lucky cousins. My parents were also visiting. We all looked at each other, realizing that we own an internet-based business. There's no reason why we couldn't move to Tennessee.

Thus began a serious conversation that resulted in all of us moving a few years later. We now all live in Tennessee as next-door neighbors, and just as we dreamed, our boys are growing up as best friends. But it didn't happen right away. We needed to find land that we all agreed was the place to put down roots. It needed to be near enough to downtown for my

sister to commute and within a specific school system. It needed to be out in the country with room for our kids to play, and it also needed to be affordable for all of us. That was a tall order in the early 2000's. It would be even more difficult today. Eventually we did find land and began to make plans to build.

One of the things I found most interesting about that time period was that once the decision had been made, my attitude and approach to life changed. Mentally and emotionally, I moved to Tennessee long before I moved physically. My future was there. My son would grow up there. I longed to begin life there.

I began to evaluate my investments in Indiana differently. I was less inclined to deepen relationships with new acquaintances because I knew I'd be moving away in the near future. We asked questions like, "Do we want to get involved in a new church if we're leaving soon?" I made business decisions with the understanding that my business was shifting locations.

I still lived in Indiana, but I was an emotional and mental resident of Tennessee.

...but our citizenship is in heaven, and we eagerly wait for a Savior from there, the Lord Jesus Christ. (Philippians 3:20)

You live here on earth right now, but your spiritual citizenship is actually in heaven. You're physically here, but Your spiritual citizenship there is both a present truth and an eternal reality.

Let's live in a way that reflects our true citizenship.

I Am a Citizen of Heaven

✠ How does your spiritual citizenship affect your current life?

✠ How should it?

✠ Is there a gap between those answers? Are there changes you need to make?

Father,

Where I live now feels so much more real to me most of the time, but I know that you've declared that I'm a citizen of heaven. That's true for eternity, but it's also true for right now. I may not be there, but my citizenship is. Thank you for that truth. I ask that you transform my life in such a way that it's evident in my values, my thoughts, and my actions.

I love you. Amen.

WEEK 08
DAY 03

One of the things that I've discovered in writing these devotions is that I'm not a deep thinker. I'm not a theologian, and I never will be. Sometimes, while doing research on a topic, I'll read background information and the depth of thought, discussion, and argument makes my head swim. For thousands of years, men have been digging into the scriptures so deeply and discussing implications and meanings so profound that I'm left wondering if I could even follow those conversations.

The scripture and topic that today's passage brings up is one of those difficult ideas. I've been reading sermons from the 1800s, commentary in random forums, and messages from current thinkers. There are a lot of deep rabbit holes we can go down with this idea, and if you're interested in that, there are a lot of people willing to dive into them with you. That's not a bad thing. Diving into deep theological waters is great. But today, instead, we're only wading.

...and if children, also heirs—heirs of God and coheirs with Christ—if indeed we suffer with him so that we may also be glorified with him. (Romans 8:17)

I Am a Coheir with Christ

As children of God, we are also God's heirs. A few years ago, my family went through the process of helping my parents create a plan for the division of their assets after their death. It wasn't the easiest experience to go through, but someday I'll be very grateful we did it so we're not making decisions in the midst of grief.

Not only will I receive physical things from my parents' estate, but I've inherited physical characteristics of each of my parents. I've inherited a family culture and family values.

As children of God, we have an inheritance much more amazing than that of any child on earth. No matter how wealthy or influential our human parents, God, as your parent has a far greater inheritance for you than any earthly parent could. But the end of that verse is a bit unsettling, yes? Our inheritance is dependent on our suffering with Christ. Matthew, Mark, and Luke all mention Jesus saying, "If anyone wants to follow after me, let him deny himself, take up his cross daily, and follow me."

> *"If the world hates you, understand that it hated me before it hated you. If you were of the world, the world would love you as its own. However, because you are not of the world, but I have chosen you out of it, the world hates you." (John 15:18-19)*

The Christian life should never be presented as easy. Jesus never indicated that belief in him would create a life free from problems. He tells us instead, that there is hope in him through and beyond our problems. When speaking on this verse, John Piper says,

I Am a Coheir with Christ

If there were no afflictions and difficulties and troubles and pain, our fallen hearts would fall ever more deeply in love with the comforts and securities and pleasures of this world instead of falling more deeply in love with our inheritance beyond this world, namely, God himself. Suffering is appointed for us in this life as a great mercy to keep us from loving this world more than we should and to make us rely on God who raises the dead. "Through many tribulations we must enter the kingdom of God" (Acts 14:22).[1]

There's a lot of deep discussion in the material I read about what exactly our inheritance is—too deep for the design of these meditations! Though this is a slightly different context than the verse is meant for, the idea is applicable, and I do know this:

> *If you then, who are evil, know how to give good gifts to your children, how much more will your Father in heaven give good things to those who ask him? (Matthew 7:11)*

Whatever the inheritance, I know the giver, and he is good. He is powerful, knowing, and loving beyond anything I am capable of understanding, even if I were the smartest, deepest-thinking theologian on earth. And if I keep my eyes and heart focused on him—despite circumstances and difficulties—if I continue to walk with my hand and heart in Christ, I am sure that inheritance will be mine someday.

I'm also sure it will be worth it, because my Father is trustworthy. And he says that I'm a coheir with his son.

I Am a Coheir with Christ

- How can understanding that you have an inheritance from God help you today?
- What are your expectations of God and your circumstances in life?
- How do you typically respond to John Piper's description of this world, "all the groaning that comes with the futility of this fallen age—persecution, calamity, disease, death?"

Father,

Thank you for being the embodiment of goodness and love, and directing those toward me. Thank you for calling me your child and promising me an inheritance alongside Christ. I ask for wisdom in dealing with all the problems I face today here on earth and look forward to the day when your inheritance makes all of those problems seem insignificant.

I love you. Amen.

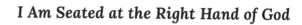

WEEK 08
DAY 04

Wikipedia says, "The Round Table is King Arthur's famed table in the Arthurian legend, around which he and his Knights congregate. As its name suggests, it has no head, implying that everyone who sits there has equal status."[1]

Why was the round table such a departure? Because formal seating etiquette has been well defined for centuries upon centuries. Guests and dignitaries are seated at formal events by rank. By importance. By positions of power and authority. The most important sit at the right hand of the leader.

> So the Lord Jesus, after speaking to them, was taken up into heaven and sat down at the right hand of God. (Mark 16:19)

> So if you have been raised with Christ, seek the things above, where Christ is, seated at the right hand of God. (Colossians 3:1)

> The Son is the radiance of God's glory and the exact expression of his nature, sustaining all things by his powerful word. After making purification for sins, he sat down at the right hand of the Majesty on high. (Hebrews 1:3)

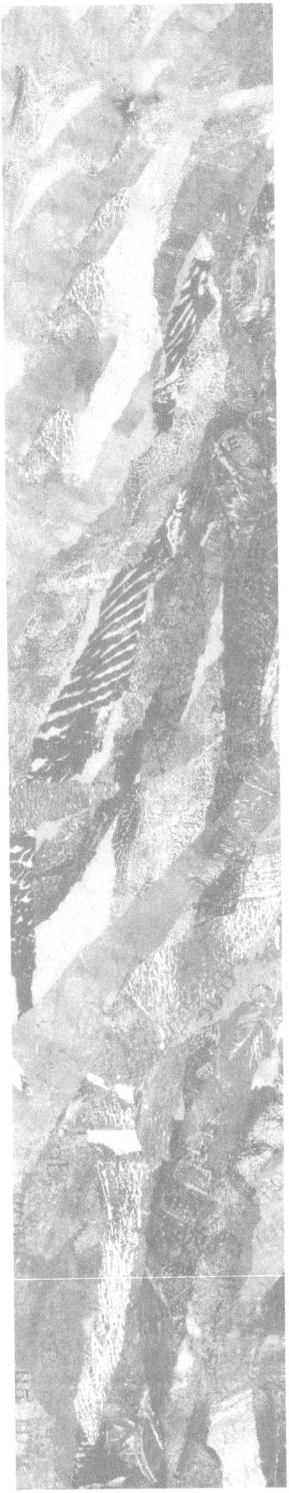

I Am Seated at the Right Hand of God

But this man, after offering one sacrifice for sins forever, sat down at the right hand of God. (Hebrews 10:12)

...keeping our eyes on Jesus, the source and perfecter of our faith. For the joy that lay before him, he endured the cross, despising the shame, and sat down at the right hand of the throne of God. (Hebrews 12:2)

As much as we, in our culture, admire equality and the idea of Arthur's round table, eternal reality is not democratic. God is the authority, the one in the position of power. Christ sits at God's right hand. And where are we?

But God, who is rich in mercy, because of his great love that he had for us, made us alive with Christ even though we were dead in trespasses. You are saved by grace! He also raised us up with him and seated us with him in the heavens in Christ. (Ephesians 2:4–6)

Spiritually, we are seated in the heavens in Christ. You are seated in the highest possible position of power. This isn't something we're working for, aiming at, or hoping to achieve. This is a completed task. Already done. This is your present spiritual reality.

- Why is this meaningful?
- What does being seated with Christ at the right hand of God make possible?

I Am Seated at the Right Hand of God

✤ What does it say about you?

✤ What practical difference does this make in your life?

Father,

Thank you for every spiritual blessing you've given us, those that we understand and those that we don't. Thank you for the honors and privileges you've given us that we don't deserve. Help us to understand the reality of being seated in Christ at your right hand, what it means for us and how we should respond.

I love you. Amen.

WEEK 08
DAY 05

In 2015, a 29-year-old American woman was attacked through a car window and killed by a female African lion. The guide in the car with her tried to fight the lion off, suffering injuries in the process. The lion was eventually chased off, and despite prompt response from the local ambulance, sadly, the woman died.[3]

The incident happened on a car tour of a lion reserve. While signs were posted throughout the park not to roll car windows down, she had done so in order to take photos.[4] Lions are accomplished hunters. Their claws are the length of a human finger. They have viciously sharp teeth.[5] They rely on short bursts of speed and immense strength. Their tongues are rough, covered with small spines which face backward. If a lion licked your arm, it could quickly scrape the flesh from your body.[6] They live at the top of the food chain in Africa and are a formidable predator.

> Be sober-minded, be alert. Your adversary the devil is prowling around like a roaring lion, looking for anyone he can devour. (1 Peter 5:8)

Had the American tourist been sober-minded and alert to the danger around her, she might

be alive today. She was warned. No one tours a lion reserve without being aware there are lions present. But she treated the experience like a Disney theme park rather than a potential murder scene.

We also have been warned. We have a very real enemy present in the world. While it's easy to become consumed with life as usual, don't let your guard down. There's a prowling lion looking to devour you. Let me say that again to be clear. You have a mortal enemy looking to destroy you if possible.

This is not an adorable grown-up cartoon Simba. This is a powerfully strong hunter. A skilled predator. And he is perpetually hunting you. Lions hunt mostly at night and use both cooperative measures and ambush tactics to seize prey. They are incredibly good at hiding and are phenomenally patient.[7] Think about how those tactics might be used against you. I think it's possible to push this analogy too far, but I want you to understand that whether you're taking your kids to school, watching a movie, or hard at work at your job, you belong to the kingdom of God and that means that you do have a spiritual enemy.

> *He has rescued us from the domain of darkness and transferred us into the kingdom of the Son he loves. (Colossians 1:13)*

The devil wants to destroy all that is God's, and you belong to God. You have an enemy.

✤ What does it look like on a practical level to be spiritually sober-minded and alert?

✤ How aware are you that you have a very real spiritual enemy?

✤ What implications does this have for your identity?.

Father,

Help me understand how to be sober-minded and alert at all times. Help me be aware that I have a real enemy. Grow me in spiritual strength, connection to other believers, and dependence on you. I thank you that I belong to you.

I love you. Amen

WEEK 08
DAY 06

Most National Football League linemen weigh over 300 pounds and are more than 6'-3" tall. They're typically the tallest, heaviest, and strongest men on the field. However, even quarterbacks have an average height of 6'-3", according to Pro-Football-Reference.com. These are not small men. They're not even average-sized men—the average height of an American male is 5'-9".

This means there are 22 human monster trucks in helmets rowdying around on the field at any given time during a game. The whistle used by most refs fits in the palm of your hand, yet can be heard without amplification a mile away. If an average-sized guy in black and white stripes blows that small whistle, all the monster trucks come to a halt, play stops, and they listen.

Therefore, submit to God. Resist the devil, and he will flee from you. (James 4:7)

Yes, we do have an enemy, and he is strong. But like the average guy in stripes with a hella loud whistle has the authority to limit the actions of football players much bigger and stronger than he, so we have the authority to limit Satan's activity in our lives.

I Have Authority over Satan

Satan opposes God, and he seeks to destroy all that belongs to God. But God is sovereign over all things, including Satan. Satan is on a leash, so to speak. God must have a purpose in allowing Satan to do his thing, otherwise he'd throw him into the lake of fire now rather than later.

Understand that we have an enemy, but he is limited and he will be destroyed in the end (see Revelation 20:10). Scripture is available to learn his tactics, prayer is available to obtain help at all times, and God has given us an action plan in James 4:7, quoted above. Submit to God. Resist the devil.

✤ What are a few practical ways you can submit to God?

✤ What are a few practical ways you can resist Satan?

✤ How does today's topic apply to your identity?

Father,

Satan is real. Your Word says so and I believe you. You say he's prowling around like a roaring lion and looking to steal, kill, and destroy. I believe you. You say he's my enemy and I believe you. You are with me and you have all authority over him. You say that I also have authority over him. You hold me securely. I believe you.

I Have Authority over Satan

Teach me to discern the activities of the enemy and give me ever-growing, ever-deepening submission to you.

I love you. Amen.

WEEK 08
DAY 07

This week, we've looked at how your spiritual citizenship affects your life. We learned that you are a citizen of heaven, a coheir with Christ, and you are seated at the right hand of God. We learned that you have an enemy over whom you have authority.

What has God spoken to your heart this week?

How have these truths changed the way you think or feel about yourself?

Father,

Help me understand how my spiritual citizenship needs to affect my behavior, my mindset, and my understanding of who I am. The idea that I'm a coheir with Christ and seated with him at the right hand of God can be strange and difficult to fathom. Help me understand what that means for me. Help me live with an appropriate awareness of my spiritual enemy and the right mindset about my authority over him.

I love you. Amen.

Next week, we'll look at the purposes God has for you. Certainly, he has created you for specific reasons, but he's outlined purposes that apply to all believers as well. Do you know what they are?

WHAT DOES GOD SAY ABOUT MY PURPOSE?

WEEK 09

WEEK 09
DAY 01

In the first two-thirds of this book, we've focused on what God says about who you are. This week we're going to shift gears a bit and begin looking at what God has to say about what those truths mean about your place in the world.

This week, we'll look at your purpose. We know from Ephesians 2:10 that God had specific plans in mind when he created each of us.

For we are his workmanship, created in Christ Jesus for good works, which God prepared ahead of time for us to do.

But our purpose isn't just individual. There are general purposes that all believers are destined for as well. This week, we'll look at the following:

✽ I am the salt of the earth.

✽ I am the light of the world.

✽ I am a stranger, an exile.

✽ I am a fountain of living water.

✽ I am God's worker.

What Does God Say About My Purpose?

PRAY

Father,

Knowing my purpose is so helpful in understanding how to live my life. As I read in the coming week, give me understanding and wisdom to absorb these purposes into my heart. Let these purposes become so much a part of my attitudes and actions that they are the hallmark of my life.

I love you. Amen.

MEDITATION VERSE

Think about this verse throughout the week. Write it on a sticky note and leave it where you'll see it often. Or, go to **www.whogodsaysyouare.link/resources** and download the pdf with the weekly meditation verses. Print and hang the appropriate verse for each week where you'll see it often. Found in the same online resource list, you'll find a guide for meditating on scripture that will explain what it means to meditate on scripture, what it doesn't mean and offer suggestions.

Dear Friends,
I URGE YOU AS STRANGERS AND EXILES TO ABSTAIN FROM SINFUL DESIRES THAT WAGE WAR AGAINST THE SOUL. CONDUCT YOURSELVES HONORABLY AMONG THE GENTILES, SO THAT WHEN THEY SLANDER YOU AS EVILDOERS, THEY WILL OBSERVE YOUR GOOD WORKS AND WILL glorify GOD ON THE DAY HE VISITS.

1 Pe 2:11-12

WEEK 09
DAY 02

I love salt. My favorite part of a pretzel bag is the salt and crumbs leftover in the bottom. It seems like there should be a weird dictionary word for that, but I can't find one. Salted caramel is always better than regular-plain-ole' caramel. My favorite moments of breakfast? The salt leftover on the plate after I've eaten eggs. My favorite steak topping? You guessed it. Salt. Salt enhances flavor.

Salting food is also one of the oldest forms of preservation. Most bacteria, fungi, and other potentially dangerous organisms can't live in a highly salty environment; they die or become inactive due to dehydration.[1] Refrigeration wasn't common until the 1920s and '30's, so in the first century in the Middle East, salt was critical in keeping food from decay.

"You are the salt of the earth. But if the salt should lose its taste, how can it be made salty? It's no longer good for anything but to be thrown out and trampled under people's feet." (Matthew 5:13)

As a Christ-follower, Matthew says you are the salt of the earth. His original readers would have known salt as both a flavor-enhancer and a

preservative. Christians both enrich the culture they're in and preserve it from decay.

Salt doesn't have to try to enhance flavor. Flavor is enhanced simply because that's the nature of salt. It doesn't have to work hard to preserve food from decay. Food is preserved because that's the nature of salt.

When we read this passage and others like it, our reaction is often to think about what we can do to be salt in our world. We read it as a call to action. But that misses the point. The important thing to remember is that your "saltiness," your ability to enrich and preserve, comes from Christ in you. It springs from your relationship with your Heavenly Father.

Be less concerned about trying to be salt and more concerned about seeking after Christ. The more you seek after Christ and fall in love with him, the saltier you will be, simply by your nature.

- In what ways do Christians preserve the world from decay?
- In what ways do Christians enhance the world?
- How salty are you in the world right now?
- How could you lose your saltiness?

I Am the Salt of the Earth

Father,

Help me seek after you more and more intently. Draw my heart into a deeper and deeper relationship with you. Keep me from diluting your presence in my life with distractions, idols, or sin. Be visible in my life to preserve, protect, and enhance the world around me.

I love you. Amen.

WEEK 09
DAY 03

One of my friends posted on social media the other day that the only thing they've seen recently that gives them hope for America is the new season of *Queer Eye*.

Let that sink in for a few moments.

Queer Eye, or any other show, being the only hope for our country is a frightening statement. There are vast numbers of disillusioned people in America right now. Their politician wasn't elected. Or, he/she was and isn't what they'd hoped. I happened to catch the nightly news by accident the other night: four different shootings in my city overnight. I don't live in New York City or Los Angeles. If four shootings overnight are normal for my area, then I've been away from the news longer than I realized.

School shootings, racial tensions, and white supremacy marches. A September 2017 report from the International Labor Organization and Walk Free Foundation estimated that there are currently almost 25 million victims of human trafficking globally, including both sex and labor trades. Twenty-five million. Almost three-quarters of those are women and girls. A quarter of them are children. I could go on with statistics and examples until my fingers

can't type anymore.

There is an incredible amount of darkness in the world.

> I have come as light into the world, so that everyone who believes in me would not remain in darkness. (John 12:46)

There is darkness, but there is light also. And it's not found on *Queer Eye*, or from politicians, or even from social workers or people working hard against the darkness.

> Jesus spoke to them again: "I am the light of the world. Anyone who follows me will never walk in the darkness but will have the light of life." (John 8:12)

Christ alone is the light of the world. And because you are in Christ, you are also the light of the world.

> "You are the light of the world. A city situated on a hill cannot be hidden. No one lights a lamp and puts it under a basket, but rather on a lampstand, and it gives light for all who are in the house. In the same way, let your light shine before others, so that they may see your good works and give glory to your Father in heaven." (Matthew 5:14-16)

When the darkness seems overwhelming, remember that it's in darkness that light is most visible. A candle in the sunshine still offers warmth and light, but it has a much bigger impact in the darkness.

Just like salt, we don't work at being light. We

work at seeking Christ. We work at keeping our eyes on him. We work at submitting to him, obeying him, and worshiping him. Then his light will shine brightly in us

✤ Where do you tend to look for light in this dark world?

✤ From these verses, where is it found?

✤ From Matthew 5:16, what's the purpose of the light in you?

✤ What dims the light of Christ in you?

Father,

Help me not to place my hope in people and things that fade away, but to place it in you alone. When I feel overwhelmed by darkness, remind me your light cannot go out. Show me ways that I'm dimming or hiding your light in me. May any light that shines in my life bring glory not to me, but to you.

I love you. Amen.

WEEK 09
DAY 04

Last Spring, I went to Greece and spent a few days working with some local churches who minister to the refugee population in Athens. The refugee crisis in Greece is far from resolved, despite it falling off of the international news radar. There are still regular reports of horrific conditions in camps across Greece, mostly due to overcrowding. There just isn't space to hold the number of people living in the camps.

Most refugee waves in history have been somewhat homogeneous, but not this one. It consisted of a wide variety of nationalities, languages, customs, and therefore, tensions.

The refugees were looking for a way out of terrible conditions and were told they would find a future in Greece. Generally, they've been lied to, manipulated, swindled, and dumped. They arrive in Greece with an 18-month wait for a visa (At least that was the time frame when I was there, and it had improved from the 24 months it had been.), no way to earn a living (You need a visa to be employed or travel outside Greece.), with no ability to speak the language, and with no where else to go. We were told that these refugees weren't typically poor. They were often skilled and educated,

tradespeople and professionals in their own country.

If you're reading this, odds are you're a native of the land you live in. It's likely that you speak the language of your home country and you're probably working and earning a living.

Dear friends, I urge you as strangers and exiles to abstain from sinful desires that wage war against the soul. (1 Peter 2:11)

If you're a Christian, the reality is that you're living the life of a refugee, or exile. Just like the Yugoslavian, Afghan, and Syrian refugees I worked with, you're living in a land which is not your home. Generally, refugees have fled their homes due to famine, war, persecution, or natural disaster. You haven't fled your home, but you aren't able to live there either.

Friends, this world is not your home, so don't make yourselves cozy in it. Don't indulge your ego at the expense of your soul. Live an exemplary life among the natives so that your actions will refute their prejudices. Then they'll be won over to God's side and be there to join in the celebration when he arrives. (1 Peter 2:11-12 MSG)

Because we value different things than our culture does, because we make decisions differently, because our priorities are different, there are times when you're going to feel out of place in this culture. I want to remind you today that it's okay to feel that way. You are an exile here. Christ in you is here to dispel the darkness in the world, and if you looked, acted, and felt

like that darkness, you would be part of it. So be encouraged by the differences. Fitting in is not your goal.

✤ Have you ever felt like an alien, a refugee, or an exile?

✤ How does knowing you're supposed to feel like that change things?

✤ What practical implications does it have?

Father,

It is so easy for me to get cozy in this world, to adopt its values and dilute my saltiness or light. Forgive me for holding so tightly to the things of this world. Remind me continually that it's not my home. Help me remember that my real citizenship is in heaven and help me act accordingly. Encourage me in my different-ness and help me be an encouragement to others.

I love you. Amen.

WEEK 09
DAY 05

Next to a well, Jesus shares with a Samaritan woman (who would have been hated by the Jews of her time) that he was the Jewish Messiah, come to save all people for all time.

Jesus answered, "If you knew the gift of God, and who is saying to you, 'Give me a drink,' you would ask him, and he would give you living water."... Jesus said, "Everyone who drinks from this water will get thirsty again. But whoever drinks from the water that I will give him will never get thirsty again. In fact, the water I will give him will become a well of water springing up in him for eternal life." (John 4:10, 13-14)

Here are five facts about water and corresponding spiritual truths:

✤ A person can live about a month without food, but only about a week without water.[2] *Water is absolutely critical to our survival, both physical and spiritual.*

✤ Water makes up about 66% of the human body and 70% of the human brain.[3] *We are made in the image of God and He calls himself living water.*

I Am a Fountain of Living Water

✣ Water can dissolve more substances than any other liquid, including sulfuric acid.[4] *Living water dissolves hardened, sin-filled hearts. It's the only thing that can do so.*

✣ Unsafe water kills 200 children every hour.[5] *Apart from the living water of Christ, we are lost. People die daily, not having drunk from this water.*

✣ In some countries, less than half the population has access to clean water.[6] *There are many who don't know, haven't heard that Jesus is the living water that they need.*

The one who believes in me, as the Scripture has said, will have streams of living water flow from deep within him. (John 7:38)

If you drink deeply from the living water, not only will you never be thirsty again, but you become a fountain yourself of living water.

Becoming a Christ-follower is not merely a decision to believe in a set of facts. When you accept his sacrifice on your behalf, you receive a never-ending supply of living water welling up inside of you. It's a fountain in the desert. The one who creates that never-ending, life-giving fountain lives inside of you and wants you to revel in that abundance for eternity.

I Am a Fountain of Living Water

✤ Do you think of Christ's living water as crucial for your survival?

✤ Do your actions agree?

✤ Do you feel as though streams of living water flow from within you?

✤ Why or why not?

✤ How does this relate to your identity?

Father,

You tell us amazing things. You speak to us; you love on us when we aren't in a right relationship to you. The woman at the well wasn't following you, wasn't important in the world's eyes, and yet you revealed so much of who you are to her. Thank you for caring for us before we knew you. For sharing of yourself with people who don't deserve it. Thank you for providing water to quench our spiritual thirst for all eternity. And thank you for putting your life inside us with such generosity that it overflows.

I love you. Amen.

WEEK 09
DAY 06

My son and I planted a garden last spring. We've been trying to get a small kitchen garden going in an area outside our patio doors. There's barely a fistful of good soil anywhere in our yard, and this space seems to be worse than most. I planted some tomato and pepper plants, and he planted some pole bean seeds.

We planned. We each planted. I watered the plants, and we both weeded. And the garden grew. Was I responsible for that growth? Was my son? No. We helped make the conditions right for that growth to happen. We cared for the seeds and the plants. But the growth really wasn't our doing. We worked with God to make it possible, but he's what really turned the potential of those seeds into plants that would nourish my family.

After all, who is Apollos? Who is Paul? We are only God's servants through whom you believed the Good News. Each of us did the work the Lord gave us. I planted the seed in your hearts, and Apollos watered it, but it was God who made it grow. It's not important who does the planting, or who does the watering. What's important is that God makes the seed

grow. The one who plants and the one who waters work together with the same purpose. And both will be rewarded for their own hard work. For we are both God's workers. And you are God's field. You are God's building. (1 Corinthians 3:5-9 NLT)

Plants grew. We ate nourishing beans, tomatoes, and peppers. In true teen fashion, early enthusiasm faded with the weed growth and soaring summer temperatures, but we both cared for the plants. He planted, and I weeded. But the growth, really neither of us can be credited with. God designed those plants, that food. He makes it grow. It doesn't really matter which of us weeded more. We worked together and cooperated with God to create the harvest.

We are each God's workers in this world. We help make conditions right for God to do his work here. But, ultimately he creates the growth and harvest. He creates the spiritual fruit in our lives and the lives of those around us.

✤ Do you think of yourself as partnering with God to do his work? Why or why not?

✤ Do you ever take credit for things that God really accomplishes?

✤ How good of a spiritual teammate are you? Do you care more about God's results or your effort on his behalf?

I Am God's Worker

Father,

Please forgive me for any time I try to take credit for something you've done. Help me work alongside other Christians with a heart that is more concerned with your glory than my own. You grow what you want in the world in miraculous ways. Grow the fame of your name and let me be a part of it in any way you want.

I love you. Amen.

WEEK 09
DAY 07

This week, we've looked at God's purposes for his children. We discovered that we're intended to be the salt of the earth, a light in the dark, a stranger in our land, a fountain of living water, and his worker.

What has God spoken to your heart this week?

How have these truths changed the way you think or feel about yourself?

Father,

I cannot accomplish these purposes without your Holy Spirit. Guide, direct, and encourage me as I take steps to live out these purposes in my life. Help me see the parts of my life that need to change. Keep me from trying to fulfill these purposes in my own strength and abilities, and instead, teach me to rely on you. Draw me closer and closer to you.

I love you. Amen.

We all play a variety of roles in our life, and becoming a believer brings with it some specific roles. Next week, we'll discover what those are.

WHAT ARE THE RESULTS OF MY IDENTITY?

WEEK 10

WEEK 10
DAY 01

If you're a mom, you'll probably experience most of the following roles in life: daughter, friend, parent, nurse, teacher, disciplinarian, counselor, taxi-driver, bank, advice columnist, cook, cat herder, maid, organizer, planner, judge, and butler. We fulfill an incredible number of roles in our lives, in our work, home, family, and community.

Some of those roles are dictated by circumstances and some by choice. Some roles we enjoy and others we don't. Some roles are optional, and some are just part of life.

Life as a Christ-follower is no different. Christ transforms some of the roles we already have in life, and there are others that we all share. This week we'll look at these roles we play:

✛ I am a prisoner of Christ.

✛ I am a sheep.

✛ I am a witness.

✛ I am a soldier.

✛ I am an ambassador.

PRAY

Father,

Help me understand how you impact all the roles in my life. I choose to let you permeate all of them. Help me understand this week the roles you've given to me as a believer and help me know the steps I need to take to step into those roles.

I love you. Amen.

MEDITATION VERSE

Think about this verse throughout the week. Write it on a sticky note and leave it where you'll see it often. Or, go to **www.whogodsaysyouare.link/resources** and download the pdf with the weekly meditation verses. Print and hang the appropriate verse for each week where you'll see it often. Found in the same online resource list, you'll find a guide for meditating on scripture that will explain what it means to meditate on scripture, what it doesn't mean and offer suggestions.

I am THE GOOD SHEPHERD. *I know* MY OWN, *& my own* KNOW ME.

JOHN 10:14

WEEK 10
DAY 02

I made a mistake when I started writing today's topic. I began researching prison stories. I looked at what prison life was like in the first century. I read prison stories from current news reports. I read stories from Nazi concentration camps. Some of those stories were inspiring. Some made the reality of human sinful nature more real than it has been in a long time. Either way, the stories disturbed me in a visceral way.

Did you ever take a career aptitude test in high school? Answer fifty questions and the test results will show your perfect career choice! As I had absolutely no idea what to do with my future, I eagerly filled in the little blue-edged circles with a number-two pencil. Those tests always showed that I value my autonomy and freedom more than money or status. And they were right. I do.

Prison stories prick fear in someone who's lived life far from the streets. Far from crime and punishment. They prick fear in someone who loves freedom more than money or status.

For this reason, I, Paul, the prisoner of Christ Jesus on behalf of you Gentiles. (Ephesians 3:1)

I Am a Prisoner of Christ

When Paul calls himself a prisoner of Christ, he's not using a term we want to talk about. There are hundreds of sermons available online which cover our freedom in Christ (This is a good thing.), but in my brief look this afternoon, I couldn't find any on being a prisoner of Christ.

We desperately want to hear about the freedom. Why? Because we already know what it's like to be a prisoner.

Paul knew what prison life was like. He was probably in Rome under house arrest and chained to an imperial guard when he wrote his letter to the Ephesians. He had been in prison other times in worse conditions. The believers who received this letter knew he was imprisoned because of his belief in Christ. They would expect him to say as much. But he wants to make it clear that he's not only a prisoner of Rome. He's also a prisoner of Christ.

You may not have the experience of a Nazi camp, an LA penitentiary, or a first century holding cell. But there are almost certainly things in your life which have curbed your freedom. Things which direct your actions, control your attitudes, or have trapped you in circumstances.

If you've lost control of your life to an addiction, an attitude, a circumstance, or another person, you know what it is to be a prisoner. I've been imprisoned by depression, perfectionism, and fear. I've been imprisoned by greed, pride, self-love, and success. I'm not comparing my prisons to anyone else's. Admittedly, some are easier than others. The comfortable ones may be more pleasant, but are no less real. Your prisons might not look like mine. But I'll bet when you consider your life you'll discover that you'll have at least a few.

I Am a Prisoner of Christ

I don't trust my depression, my perfectionism, or my fear. But I trust Christ. I know that as a prisoner of Christ, I'm controlled and directed by someone who has my best interest at heart. The one who designed me for a specific role. The one who sees the big picture of redemption and how all the pieces of my life and yours fit together into that picture. The one who loved me enough to die for me.

We value our freedoms in this country. But that doesn't mean we aren't prisoners. As a believer, I owe everything to Christ. I'm willing to offer my autonomy to him, I'm willing to be captured, confined, and constrained by the one who loves me more than life. I'm willing to submit to the control of God as a prisoner of Christ.

Are you?

✤ What are you or have you been a prisoner of in your life?

✤ Can you call yourself, as Paul did, a prisoner of Christ?

✤ What aspects of your life are not under his control?

Jesus,

Some days it's easier to declare myself your prisoner. Other days I feel like a fraud when I do. But, my desire is for you to be in control.

I Am a Prisoner of Christ

Direct me and guide me. Those words are easier to say than to mean. But I owe you everything I have, and I want my attitudes, my actions, my desires to be in line with that belief. You have my submission to your authority and control of my life. Help me see the areas where I fall short in that and help me know how to bring them under your control. I trust you.

I love you. Amen.

WEEK 10
DAY 03

The lyrics to the chorus of one of my favorite children's songs[1] by Zoe Lewis are as follows:

> Well there are Border Leicesters,
> fat, fluffy
> Shetlands, Rylands, round, puffy
> Dorset Horns ruminating
> Southdowns, Romneys tails shaking
> Lincoln Longwools, shy, sweet
> Hop, skip, jump and a leap
> Everywhere I look, everyone I
> meet...SHEEP!
> Some baa, some bray some bleat...
> They're called SHEEP!

This song is a happy piece that both kids and adults can thoroughly enjoy, with lots of clever writing. The meaning of the song totally shifts for me with the line, "Everywhere I look, everyone I meet...SHEEP!"

> *All of us, like sheep, have strayed away.*
> *We have left God's paths to follow our own.*
> *Yet the Lord laid on him*
> *the sins of us all. (Isaiah 53:6 NLT)*

Would you choose to describe yourself as a sheep? If you're not familiar with their

characteristics beyond a barnyard animal that says, "Baaaa," let me help you out with a few details.

Sheep are gregarious and social in nature. They're programmed to hang out in a herd. Their instincts frequently override their limited intelligence. They produce wool, simply by being alive. Domesticated sheep do not do well on their own, separated from human owners. They are defenseless and easily disturbed. They do not hear or see very well and have no sense of direction. They follow one another blindly and are prone to stray. They are affectionate and learn to respond to their shepherd's voice. They are picky eaters, foolish, slow learners, awkward, stubborn, demanding, unpredictable, and dependent on their caretakers.

What an analogy! This isn't how people would typically describe themselves. We don't like to think of ourselves as defenseless, dependent, foolish, slow learners, and awkward. We like to think of ourselves as strong, smart, self-sufficient, independent, and brave.

But God calls us sheep.

This is an incredibly rich analogy, but today let's just think about it in two ways. First, God calls us sheep. So we need to understand ourselves that way even if we prefer not to.

Second, sheep are lost without a shepherd. And God says that he is our true shepherd.

The Lord is my shepherd;
I have what I need. (Psalm 23:1)

I am the good shepherd. The good shepherd lays down his life for the sheep. (John 10:11)

I am the good shepherd. I know my own, and

my own know me, just as the Father knows me, and I know the Father. I lay down my life for the sheep. (John 10:14-15)

Pastor and author Skip Heitzig says:

> As a shepherd himself, David knew that the quality of life for any sheep depends on the kind of shepherd who takes care of it...There's a secret to being a happy sheep. If you stay at a distance from your Shepherd, wander around, and find your own way, "Happy" won't be your nickname. Remember, happiness and safety are directly proportional to proximity. The closer you live to your Shepherd, the more you will be nourished and cared for by Him, and safe because of His protection.[2]

The qualities of a sheep may not appeal to us, but they appeal to God. He wants us close. He wants us dependent. He wants us listening and looking to him.

✤ What do you learn about yourself from the characteristics of sheep?

✤ How do you feel about being called a sheep?

✤ How well do you know your shepherd's voice?

✤ What would help you stay in close proximity to your shepherd this week?

I Am a Sheep

Father,

I'm a sheep, and I'm made to be dependent on a shepherd. Help me always stay close to you, to treat you as my true shepherd. Help me not be dependent on lesser things. Help me not to "nibble myself lost" as one of my former pastors used to say. Thank you for your shepherding me well, for laying down your life for me.

I love you. Amen.

WEEK 10
DAY 04

I spent eighteen months fostering dogs. Big dogs. Little dogs. Sick dogs. Healthy dogs (well, as healthy as a dog needing foster care can be). Some of our foster dogs stayed with us for a weekend and some for months at a time. The very last dog we fostered was named Wylie.

If I remember correctly, I was Wylie's sixth home in about as many months. He'd had a rough go of it. By the time he got to me, he was a real problem. He'd been left on a chain with no food or water for extended periods. He was a high-strung escape artist who couldn't be left alone. When he was alone and he couldn't escape from his home or yard, he became destructive. He'd been kicked out of his doggie daycare facility for getting in a fight with a comrade over food. He'd shredded curtains and furniture. He'd routinely been jumping a six-foot fence.

I was somewhat of a last-ditch effort at rehabilitation. He spent the first four months on lockdown. He didn't eat, sit, lay down, walk, move, or drink without my permission. He learned to stay where I put him, look to me for permission to do anything, and work for his food. He learned to hang out in a crate (relatively) peacefully. He learned basic obedience and how to handle my leaving and returning. None of

this was easy. None of it was a whole lot of fun for either one of us. But it's how a crazy dog is transformed into a healthy pet.

Most people think fostering is about loving on animals who need love. They imagine couch cuddles, toys, and kisses. But love and freedom is not how traumatized pups are transformed into healthy family members. Structure, discipline, reward, workouts, and training have a much bigger impact than human affection.

Not that I didn't love Wylie. I loved him enough that he ended my foster career. Four years later, he's a legitimate family member with full couch privileges. He still carries scars (don't we all?), but he just stepped voluntarily into his crate to lay down as I type, and he rarely shows his former crazy-dog-self anymore.

I get into a lot of conversations about dogs. A lot of conversations with families who have problems with their own pups. When they hear Wy's story of going from a half-starved crate destroyer to a voluntary crate relaxer, they want to know how I did it. They want to know how a high-strung pup with severe separation anxiety turned into a companion who often elicits the phrase, "He's so calm!" upon introduction.

And I tell them. I tell them time, structure, control, and consistency. I can tell them with authority because I've seen it work. I've seen it work in other families. I've known of other hard cases where it's worked. But my authority rests on the fact that it's our story. It's our experience. You may disagree. You may believe that affection and snuggles rehabilitate dogs, but you can't dispute our success.

I Am a Witness

"But you will receive power when the Holy Spirit has come on you, and you will be my witnesses in Jerusalem, in all Judea and Samaria, and to the end of the earth." (Acts 1:8)

God says that you're to be a witness. You're to tell people about God everywhere. We often think of witnessing as a big event. Something the super-spiritual do, those gifted in evangelism, or those called to be missionaries. But that's not what this verse says. A witness isn't someone who has a degree in religious studies. It's not someone who needs to be able to explain the Trinity, predestination, or the order of events in Revelation. It's not someone who can stand before a classroom of students and teach apologetics.

A witness is someone who sees or experiences something and tells someone else about it. We're to simply tell people everywhere what we've experienced of God. I tell people in all types of situations about the transformation of my formerly crazy, rescued Boxer dog. In the checkout line at the grocery, chatting while serving at church, out to lunch with friends– wherever the conversation naturally lands on our pets. I can tell people about my experiences with God in the very same places.

You don't have to convince anyone to believe that God exists. That's not your job. That's the job of the Holy Spirit. Your job is to be a witness to what God's done in your life this year, this week, or this morning, sharing your experience in a natural conversation.

I Am a Witness

✤ How do you generally think about Christian witnessing?

✤ The paragraphs above assume you have daily or weekly experiences of God. Is that true for you? If not, how could that happen?

✤ If you told someone today about what God spoke to you about this topic, what would you say?

Father,

So often we make things harder than they are. Forgive us for using that as an excuse for disobedience. So often we rely on our own power when clearly, you've said in the verse above, we're to do this by the power of the Holy Spirit. Help us to begin to recognize when we have an opportunity to share something in conversation, give us the courage to do so, and the words to speak. Help us use our words to give life, give encouragement, give hope, and give love.

I love you. Amen.

WEEK 10 DAY 05

It's loud. Ridiculously so. There are so many different sounds happening at once. Rounds going out, rounds coming in. Rockets and grenades and 40mm. On top of that you're trying to communicate what you see with everyone around you. Your boss is trying to coordinate movement and fire. You go into sensory overload. Your body is pumping adrenaline like nobodies [sic] business. And through all this you have to focus on your job. (stuka370 describing combat)[3]

Whether you realize it or not, you're in a combat situation. You're a soldier of Jesus Christ. Combat is loud, confusing, and changeable. No soldier is spending his or her time in combat thinking about the things I'm thinking about on any given Monday evening. They're worried about survival. They're worried about their friends' survival. They're worried about their mission. They're worried about their job. They're worried about their life.

Share in suffering as a good soldier of Christ Jesus. No one serving as a soldier gets entangled in the concerns of civilian life; he

seeks to please the commanding officer.
(2 Timothy 2:3-4)

In discussing why soldiers develop intensely strong bonds with each other, Robert Goepp says on Quora, "The bond in the military comes from shared adversity, MUCH time spent together, a lot of it boring with time to talk, and shared significant emotional events." While the life of a soldier might be dramatized and idealized by Hollywood, it's not fun. An anonymous answer to the same Quora question says in part, "The vast majority of time in the military you're doing things that suck with other people who are doing things that suck and these things that suck can only be truly understood by those that have done things that suck."

As a good soldier of Christ, life is not intended to completely suck. But life as a soldier also isn't about your comfort, pleasure, relaxation, development, or success. It's about your mission. Don't let yourself get tangled up with desires, goals, and activities that are of "civilian life." You're a soldier; good soldiers are more worried about doing their jobs well and pleasing their commanding officer than serving themselves.

Sharing in suffering is part of what creates bonds between soldiers, but it's also just part of the job. Christ never promised that our life following him would be easy. As a matter of fact, he promised that it won't be.

When we're thinking about who we are, we cover a lot of beautiful concepts, a lot of amazing promises and privileges God has given us about who we are. But we have responsibilities, too. It's not a rainbows-and-unicorns life. We're called to serve. And serving will be messy, scary,

disorienting, difficult, and exhausting. And that's just serving your family and friends! In whatever capacity and whatever situation you're serving, there will be combat, suffering, and sacrifice.

You are a soldier of Christ. So, go! Get about being a good soldier today! Concern yourself with your mission and your Commanding Officer.

✤ As a soldier of Christ, what is your mission?

✤ Does your mind get entangled in everyday life? Or, does it stay focused on your mission?

✤ What is one way you could seek to please God today?

Father,

Help me see my role as a soldier for you more clearly. Help me understand what that means and what you want from me. Help me step into serving, suffering, and sacrifice in ways that are pleasing to you. In big ways, maybe, but in hundreds of small ways throughout my day, also. Give me spiritual eyes to see the combat around me. Guide, protect, and equip me to be a good soldier.

I love you. Amen.

WEEK 10
DAY 06

In 1776, Benjamin Franklin was appointed the United States' first ambassador and was dispatched to Paris, France. His goal was to obtain French support for the United States in our war with Great Britain. He served brilliantly. The United States had much more in common culturally, politically, and philosophically with Britain than with the French. But we needed support in our war effort, and the French and British were sworn enemies.

In 1776, Paris was not a beautiful, romantic city. Most of the population lived in abject poverty. Streets were narrow and winding with open sewers running down their center. Even the aristocracy wore elaborate wigs on their heads which were shaved to discourage lice. Conditions for most were dismal. The government was a monarchy with strict control resting in the hands of the king.[5]

Ben Franklin was an advocate for the common man and a proponent of a republican form of government. But his mission was to represent his brand-new country in the French court and obtain an alliance with the French. To do so, he needed to focus on his mission and not be distracted by other (even good) causes.

I Am an Ambassador

Everything is from God, who has reconciled us to himself through Christ and has given us the ministry of reconciliation. That is, in Christ, God was reconciling the world to himself, not counting their trespasses against them, and he has committed the message of reconciliation to us.

Therefore, we are ambassadors for Christ, since God is making his appeal through us. We plead on Christ's behalf: "Be reconciled to God." (2 Corinthians 5:18-20)

I don't watch much television, with the exception of hockey and college football. There is some remarkably good storytelling these days, but I just don't have time. However, I'm a sucker for Mike Rowe's Facebook show, "Returning The Favor." It highlights, surprises, and helps people across the country who are doing good things in their community and helping others. "Bloody do-gooders," Mike calls them. I got sidetracked watching an episode tonight when I should have been writing.

Tonight's episode highlighted a 21-year-old woman in Greenville, South Carolina. Adah Nix does laundry once a week for the homeless and needy in her area. She was inspired to help others after finding out about her mother's homelessness as a young woman. During the episode, there was a short clip of an interview with a homeless man named Harold. One of the things he said struck me as he was describing the blessing he felt from Adah's laundry service: "Not really much people show kindness."[6]

I don't know if Adah has a spiritual basis for her kindnesses. But the world certainly needs it. "Not really much people show kindness." What an

I Am an Ambassador

incredibly sad statement to be made in a nation that has something like 240 million Christians.

Benjamin Franklin represented his government and its message in Paris in the late 1700s. His diplomacy changed the outcome of the war, making possible the country Harold and Adah live in today.

As a Christ-follower, you are an ambassador for him. You represent him to a fallen world in need of a Savior. He has shown the ultimate kindness to us. Let us remember that we are his way to show that kindness to others. And that the outcome of that diplomacy is eternal.

✤ What are some specific ways you represent Christ in your sphere of influence?

✤ What responsibilities and privileges does an ambassador have?

✤ Do you often find yourself sidetracked by other missions (even good ones)?

✤ How could you keep on track today?

Father,

You have shown me so much kindness. You've reconciled me to you through Christ and have made me your ambassador here on earth. Help me represent you well to everyone I know

and come into contact with. May the words of my mouth and the meditations of my heart be acceptable to you, Lord, my rock, and my redeemer. May my actions and attitudes in my world represent you well.

I love you. Amen.

This week, we've looked at the roles God has for us as believers. We discovered that we're prisoners of Christ, sheep, witnesses, soldiers, and ambassadors.

What has God spoken to your heart this week?

How have these truths changed the way you think or feel about yourself?

Father,

Show me very clearly the next actions I need to take to step into these roles in a deeper way. What do you want from me today? What can I do right now to follow you better as a prisoner, sheep, witness, soldier, and ambassador? Present ways in my day that I can practice these roles and give me the courage to do so.

I love you. Amen.

As we begin to live out our identity, our purposes, and our spiritual roles in the world, there are some truths that God has for us. Are you ready to learn what those are?

WHAT TRUTHS DOES GOD WANT ME TO BELIEVE?

WEEK 11

WEEK 11
DAY 01

As you begin to understand who God says you are, you'll start to see yourself, your circumstances, your life, and your priorities differently. As that happens, you may feel off balance, a bit lost, a bit found, and a bit unsure. Don't worry, you're establishing a new normal for yourself, and that takes time!

As you continue on that journey, God wants you to know a handful of things that become important as you live out your God-given identity in the world. This week, we'll look at these truths:

✤ I am a work in progress.

✤ I am part of the vine.

✤ I am more than a conqueror.

✤ I am an overcomer.

✤ I am appointed to bear fruit.

PRAY

Father,

As I step into the identity, purpose, and role you've given me, strengthen, encourage, teach, and guide me. Help me understand what I'm about to read and help me apply it in practical ways.

I love you. Amen.

MEDITATION VERSE

Think about this verse throughout the week. Write it on a sticky note and leave it where you'll see it often. Or, go to **www.whogodsaysyouare.link/resources** and download the pdf with the weekly meditation verses. Print and hang the appropriate verse for each week where you'll see it often. Found in the same online resource list, you'll find a guide for meditating on scripture that will explain what it means to meditate on scripture, what it doesn't mean and offer suggestions.

I AM THE VINE;
YOU ARE THE BRANCHES.
THE ONE WHO REMAINS IN ME.
AND I IN HIM
PRODUCES MUCH FRUIT,
because
YOU CAN DO NOTHING
WITHOUT ME.

JOHN 15:5

WEEK 11
DAY 02

I'm an artist. It has taken me years to learn not to cringe when I say that. But it's true. I just finished watching a Facebook live video of a gallery of artwork hung for a charity auction. One of the pieces on the wall is mine. Not that that is any indication of the quality of my art, but I can legitimately call myself an artist these days.

One of the things artists often do on social media is post images of partially finished pieces or "works in progress." Look up #WIP if you ever want more of that than you could wade through in a lifetime! I struggle with posting those images. A piece in progress is messy. It's unbalanced. It's not complete. It's often frustrating. It's very often nothing like how it looks when it finally ends its journey.

I struggle with sharing those points in a piece. I'd rather present the finished work to the world as if it sprang up as an already blooming daffodil in the spring (or buttercup, for my Southern friends). The hard work, the planting, fertilizing, the pushing up through the soil and the growing leaves and stems...those are an important part of the journey of the bulb on the way to the flower in bloom. A crucial and beautiful part of the story.

I constantly have to remind myself that those on-the-way moments are a critical part of the journey of every art piece as well. In my figurative collage work, I often work from a mockup using photographs. I have one sitting in my studio that's been there, prepped, waiting for several months. It's a piece that means a lot to me. It's a piece to work through grief and honor my Savior. It's in the "growing roots" stage. It's rough. It's not pretty. It's a work in progress.

Our lives are also works in progress. Paul says,

> Not that I have already reached the goal or am already perfect, but I make every effort to take hold of it because I also have been taken hold of by Christ Jesus. Brothers and sisters, I do not consider myself to have taken hold of it. But one thing I do: Forgetting what is behind and reaching forward to what is ahead, I pursue as my goal the prize promised by God's heavenly call in Christ Jesus.
> (Philippians 3:12-14)

There are moments in your journey as a believer that you will fail. You will be less than you wish you were. You will fall short. Believers still sin. In those moments, recognize that you're a work in progress. Recognize that Paul considered himself that way, too. And certainly, God is aware that you're not perfect. It's why he came. It's why he died.

I recently heard a former pastor speak from the pulpit for the first time since he'd left church leadership. He stepped out of his role as a pastor several years ago after the Holy Spirit convicted him of sin in his life. He took time away from ministry to deal with it. Friends, that man

radiated grace. I am 100% certain that his life has had rough, messy, painful moments in the last few years. But he did what Paul instructed the Philippians to do. He pressed on. John Piper says,

> The question is not whether you are perfect. Paul said, "Not that I have already obtained this or am already perfect" (3:12). Neither he nor we will be perfect in this life. The question is: Are you pressing on to make Christ your own? That is, are you resolving day by day to count Christ as your supreme treasure and count everything else as rubbish by comparison?[1]

That in-between, work-in-progress stage is where we live our whole lives here on earth. We look forward to being free from our sinful nature eventually, but as the Holy Spirit guides us into greater and greater maturity here in the meantime, know that you're a #WIP masterpiece.

❈ How does your lack of perfection affect you?

❈ What do you tend to do with the #WIP parts of your life?

❈ List three healthy things you could do with them that you aren't doing now.

❈ How does realizing we're all (including Paul) a #WIP affect your identity?

I Am a Work in Progress

Abba, Daddy,

I know I'm a work in progress and I ask you to keep guiding me into maturity. Draw my heart to hunger more and more for you. Help me love what you love, value what you value, and hate what you hate. Remind me of your grace when my imperfections loom large. Help me to forget the past and look forward to what lies ahead. Help me press on to reach the end of the race and receive the heavenly prize for which you, through Christ Jesus, are calling me.

I love you. Amen.

WEEK 11
DAY 03

I've lived in the humidity-soaked South for over a decade now and consider myself a Southerner. For those residents who would argue that I haven't been here long enough, I'll just say, "Bless their hearts," and move on. But ten years of residency still hasn't worn thin some of the amazement that wells up when faced with certain Southern charms. Like collard greens. I have nothing against collard greens, as long as they're on your plate and not mine. I'll admire them from a distance, thank you.

Another thing I'm constantly amazed at is the superhero-strength Southern weeds. They grow stronger, taller, thicker and more aggressively than this former Yankee has ever seen. I have weeds in my garden that I swear I can watch grow. Weeds that choke out any intentional plant overnight. Weeds that you pull out one morning, toss aside, and the next morning another has grown in its place, but it grew up taller and stronger in the dark of night. Weeds with an endless root system. Even the weeds take family seriously down here, intertwined with their neighbors to such a degree that you might as well dig up the whole darn yard.

I have one weed that grew to be a ten-foot tree in a few weeks' time. It grew sideways out of a

rock wall and then vertically ten feet with a trunk the size of my fist at its base. We let it grow, marveling at it daily. What we didn't realize when we watched it was that we'd be unable to get that thing out of the rock wall with any means other than dynamite (we tried). A major explosion wouldn't have been very healthy for the wall and hard to explain to the town officials, so, we had to leave the root system and about six inches of trunk in place. We cut the weed-tree down with an ax.

The nine feet of disconnected weed-tree trunk and branches roasted in the hot Tennessee sun. What had once been an aggressively healthy plant now lay starving, dying, and withering near the same rock wall where it had been rooted hours before.

"I am the true vine, and my Father is the gardener." (John 15:1)

I am the vine; you are the branches. The one who remains in me and I in him produces much fruit, because you can do nothing without me. (John 15:5)

When you and I as the branches are connected to Christ (the vine), life is fruitful. We have access to the life-giving nourishment of Christ and we naturally grow and bear fruit. When that connection is severed, we no longer have access to the source of life in Christ and we wither and die.

The weed we cut down physically died when we separated it from its life source with an ax. You may physically live when separated from Christ, but your spiritual life, your eternal impact, your ability to do anything of lasting

value, will wither and die just as surely as our nine-and-one-half-foot weed-tree leftovers did. They were strong and vibrant when connected to their source of life, but were worthless without it.

Christ is your source of life. Apart from him, you can do nothing.

✤ What one thing could you do starting today that would make the biggest difference in how connected you are to Christ?

✤ How does being part of the vine, the branches who grow fruit, affect your understanding of who you are?

Jesus,

Sometimes I'm not as connected as I should be to you, and I know that's all my own doing and not yours. Bring to my mind and heart the things that I've done that separate us and help me turn away from them. Help me constantly look to you as the source of life, as the place from which all my nourishment comes. Help me understand my separation from you as what it truly is: death. Remind me of the vine and branch analogy throughout my day today and teach me what I need to know. I'm listening.

I love you. Amen.

WEEK 11
DAY 04

I've been struggling with my schedule lately. I'm always busy—not unusual in our culture. But it's springtime in arguably the worst spot for allergies in the country, and it's crunch time at school. From Spring Break through the end of the school year is always a tough season, but I've added a trip, a class, and new business planning on top of the usual crazy. One of these years I'll learn. It was supposed to be this year.

I have done better. Even though I'm tired, I'm not really depleted. Even though I'm busy, I bounce back quickly. Even though I scheduled more than I should have, I'm not at the end of my rope. The last few years, I felt I was lucky just to get through this season. This year, I feel like I'm handling it. Coping. Slightly better than survival-mode. I always regret that this season is so crazy, because it comes immediately before my son leaves for a month to visit his dad. I'd rather have the season feel more relaxed. I'd rather we thrived.

I think in our fast-paced lives, in our competitive, comparison-centered social circles, and our always-on busyness-is-a-badge-of-honor lives that we feel like we've succeeded if nothing falls completely apart.

I Am More than a Conqueror

If there's no public crisis. If we get through
our weeks without dropping any of the really
important balls.

But is that what God wants for us?

*No, in all these things we are more than
conquerors through him who loved us.*
(Romans 8:37)

"All these things" Paul's referring to are
"tribulation, or distress, or persecution, or
famine, or nakedness, or danger, or sword."
Whatever you're struggling with, Paul says you're
more than a conqueror.

The idea that we just get by can be insidious.
We settle for a job that's unfulfilling. We settle
into poor relationship habits. We settle for
simmering in unhealthy emotions like anger,
disillusionment, or bitterness. We allow our
circumstances to set the tone for our lives.
If our life happens to be coming up roses, we
settle for comfort.

But there is so much more.

You are already more than a conqueror. Of
circumstances. Of sins. Of distress. Not because
you're amazing (which you are). Not because
you're skilled, or wise, or smart (which you may
or may not be). But because you have Christ
within you.

Thriving instead of surviving is not about
changing the circumstances you're in, not
about getting out from under persecution or
distress. Not about aiming for comfort or safety.
Instead, it's about living through Christ within
those circumstances. It's about not letting the
circumstances, whether they're good or bad,
be the measuring stick for your joy. For your

purpose. Or, for your contentment.

Because you have Christ, you are more than a conqueror. Does your life reflect that truth?

❧ Where are you settling in your life? Experiencing defeat?

❧ Where are you allowing circumstances to be the measure of your success?

❧ How does the presence of Christ available to you change your perspective in those areas?

❧ Does your life reflect the truth that you're more than a conqueror?

Father,

Forgive me for all the times I've allowed circumstances to guide my perspective. Forgive me for settling for less—less than exactly what you desire for me in my family, my relationships, my work, my life. Help me learn contentment and desire only for the things you have for me. Help me allow you to transform every area of my life into a showcase for your glory.

I love you. Amen.

WEEK 11
DAY 05

There are two sports I actually take time to watch. I do follow Indiana University basketball at a distance, but I usually only watch one or two games a year, if that. You will find me, though, watching Tennessee football in the fall and Nashville Predator hockey when I can get it. Otherwise, I listen to hockey games on the radio. Right now, the Preds are in the playoffs, and I have access to all the games. Today, I feel like that's both a blessing and a curse.

We're not playing as well in the playoffs as we played in the regular season. The first series and a half have been tight—too close for comfort. In particular, the last few games with the Winnipeg Jets (the second-best team in the league during the regular season) have been incredibly intense.

Last night's game wasn't pretty if you're a Preds fan. The first period was great. We played well, attacked early, and the Jets were off their game. When the second period started, however, the roles reversed. We lost a three-point lead and eventually lost 7-4. Preds players landed in the penalty box for much of the third period, and it was a tremendously frustrating game, a hard loss. We're now down in the series 2-1.

We finished the regular season as the best team in the NHL. But we very well may not win

the Stanley Cup. Particularly if we keep playing the way we've played most of the games in the playoffs. Just because we won the most games in the regular season, have a great goalie, and a world-class team with a lot of depth doesn't mean we'll win.

> *For this is what love for God is: to keep his commands. And his commands are not a burden, because everyone who has been born of God conquers the world. This is the victory that has conquered the world: our faith.*
> (1 John 5:3-4)

Winning championships in sports is uncertain. Even if you're good. Even if you're arguably the best. There are too many other factors at play on any given day in any given game. This is what makes it exciting to watch. Although, I'd prefer it was slightly less exciting in our favor this week!

However, in our spiritual lives, it's not like that. The most important game has already been won. Scripture says that "anyone who has been born of God overcomes the world." This is not because you scored a lot of points or stayed out of the penalty box. The victory didn't depend on your performance on any given day, in any given circumstance. Your victory over the world is given to you by your faith in the one who already won. This is a little like my Preds having wrapped up the season's standing as the number one team in the regular season while still having some games to play. We know the outcome, but we still have some challenges to overcome.

You have some challenges to overcome in this life, but by your faith in Christ, you can be sure that the ultimate challenge has already

been resolved. Because of that victory, you now have the resources to overcome all the lesser challenges along the way. Your faith gives you access to God and all of the wisdom, grace, strength, protection, steadfastness, and help you will need.

✣ Do you believe that your victory over the world is complete?

✣ Do you ever feel that sin/the world has the upper hand despite what you believe?

✣ Do your actions and attitudes reflect the truth of your victory?

✣ What actions can you take to bring your feelings and experience into agreement with the truth of 1 John 5:3-4?

Father,

Help me rest in the truth that you have already overcome the world. Let that flood my heart with peace and assurance that my game-winning performance isn't required because you've already done that. I believe that you are who you say you are and you've done what you say you've done. I believe that you shelter me safely under your wing and that you will bring everything to pass that you've promised. I trust

I Am an Overcomer

that when you say you've overcome sin and the world in my life, you have. Draw me closer to you. Help me desire you more than things of the world. Let my heart long for you more than anything else. Let my eyes and heart be so filled with you that sin is unappealing and hateful. Let my life be evidence that you've overcome the world.

I love you. Amen.

WEEK 11
DAY 06

Have you ever tracked your time? If you've ever had to bill your hours for a job, you know it can be a pain in the neck. About a year ago, I did an experiment and tracked all my time for a week. I wanted to get a grasp on how much time I was spending on projects like writing and podcasting.

What would you find if you tracked every minute of every day? I was surprised at how much time I spent in the car, how much time I frittered away doing nothing, and how much time I wasted online and on social media. I'm sure you'd have some surprises, too.

> You did not choose me, but I chose you.
> I appointed you to go and produce fruit
> and that your fruit should remain, so that
> whatever you ask the Father in my name, he
> will give you. (John 15:16)

I have apples, bananas, and the tops of about eight strawberries on my counter right now. Apparently, after I went to bed last night, my son decided he needed some strawberries, but he didn't need to clean up after himself. I can guarantee you that if we don't eat that fruit and clean up the mess, there will be rotten food on my counter shortly. Rotten fruit and a zillion

gnats. Not a pleasant thought. It's a fact of life: fruit doesn't last, it rots.

The most important thing I learned from my time-tracking experiment was how little of my time I spend on things that last. My Instagram feed won't last. My business won't last. My endless trips to the school won't last. My novel-reading won't last. My grocery shopping won't last. Most of my time is spent on things that will disappear forever.

Do you need to do some of those things without eternal significance? Yes. But if you want your time here to have an impact, to mean something, you need to invest it in lasting fruit.

I've been created to produce lasting fruit.

I've been chosen to produce lasting fruit.

I've been appointed to produce lasting fruit.

And I need to spend more of my time doing just that. But we know that fruit rots. So let's think about what lasting fruit would be. It certainly wouldn't be anything coming from the natural world, because as the strawberry remains on my counter are beginning to remind me, fruit doesn't last.

In verses one and two of this chapter, John calls God the gardener, Christ the vine, and believers the branches on the vine. He reminds us to abide in Christ, and if we do so, we'll bear much fruit. Fruit is a natural outgrowth of the nourishment and resources coming through the branches from the vine.

"I have loved you even as the Father has loved me. Remain in my love." (John 15:9)

He tells us to abide in Christ. He tells us to remain in his love. We receive love through the vine and the lasting fruit we bear is love as well.

I Am Appointed to Bear Fruit

Three things will last forever—faith, hope, and love—and the greatest of these is love.
(1 *Corinthians* 13:13)

We aren't told to work at making fruit. We're told to abide in Christ, to remain in his love. If we do so, the natural product of that relationship will be love, a fruit that lasts.

- How much of your time is invested in things that last?
- You've been appointed to bear fruit as a natural outgrowth of your relationship with Christ. How does this affect how you invest your time?
- How does the idea that you've been appointed to bear fruit change how you think about yourself and your daily activities?

Jesus,

Draw me to you and hold me tightly. Your love is the most real thing I can imagine, and yet, because my senses don't necessarily register it, it's so hard to cling to at times. Give me the faith I need to walk in obedience. Give me wisdom in the choices I make about my time today. Help me see the things in my life and schedule that need to be changed. Help me see ways I can more

I Am Appointed to Bear Fruit

consistently, more fully, more deeply, and more intentionally abide in you and remain in your love. Grow me in ways that the fruit I bear won't rot, but instead, last forever.

I love you. Amen.

WEEK 11
DAY 07

This week, we looked at truths God has for us on our journey into living out who he's created us to be. We realized that we are works in progress, part of the vine, more than conquerors, overcomers, and appointed to bear fruit.

What has God spoken to your heart this week?

How have these truths changed the way you think or feel about yourself?

Father,

Sink the seeds of these truths deep into my heart and grow them there. As I travel the journey into who you've made me to be, remind me when I need reminding that I need to abide in you, I'm a work in progress, I'm a conqueror, and an overcomer. Remind me that you've appointed me to bear fruit—that's my destiny. Grow me in ways that are pleasing to you.

I love you. Amen.

We've looked at who God says we are, the purposes and roles he's given us. As we head into the last week of reading, we'll look at why we can trust that these things will never change.

HOW SECURE IS
MY IDENTITY?

WEEK 12

WEEK 12
DAY 01

Our lives are uncertain. We lose jobs, marriages, family, and friends. Accidents happen and plans don't go as planned. Things change. Things always change. We think that's a fact of modern life, but the familiar phrase, "The only constant is change," actually dates back to a Greek philosopher.

As we finish up this look at who God says we are, it's worth reminding ourselves that our experience in life tells us that things change. But that's not true of God. God is unchanging. He spoke these truths into existence and they are permanent. This week, we'll look at how you, your position, your benefits, and your identity are secure. We'll read:

✤ I have received the Holy Spirit.

✤ I am sheltered.

✤ I am protected from stumbling.

✤ I am guarded.

✤ I am hidden.

PRAY

Father,

Remind me this week how deep your love is for me. Remind me of your power, your permanence, and your care and concern for my welfare. Teach me to trust you.

I love you. Amen.

MEDITATION VERSE

Think about this verse throughout the week. Write it on a sticky note and leave it where you'll see it often. Or, go to **www. whogodsaysyouare. link/resources** and download the pdf with the weekly meditation verses. Print and hang the appropriate verse for each week where you'll see it often. Found in the same online resource list, you'll find a guide for meditating on scripture that will explain what it means to meditate on scripture, what it doesn't mean and offer suggestions.

I HAVE BEEN crucified with Christ AND I NO LONGER LIVE — BUT CHRIST LIVES IN ME. the life I now live in the body. I LIVE BY FAITH — IN THE SON OF GOD. who loved me AND GAVE HIMSELF FOR ME.

GALATIONS 2:10

WEEK 12
DAY 02

Have you ever been rooting for the basketball team who had been winning, until they were beaten by a full-court Hail Mary shot at the buzzer? Shock. What just happened? How could it be?

Can you imagine thinking you were walking with the son of God until he was killed at the hands of a mob? How could that happen?

Last week was Holy Week in the Christian calendar. Jesus entered Jerusalem hailed as a hero, and within a week the crowds demanded his life. He suffered immense physical pain, betrayal by his closest friends, and an excruciating death. For the first time in history, the Trinity was separated. His Father withdrew from him. Christ became the guilt of the whole human race, including yours and mine, and suffered the punishment that we deserve.

At his death, his family, friends, and disciples didn't understand that our Easter was about to happen. They were grieving. Their leader, teacher, and friend was gone. Have you ever lost a loved one? A close family member? Grief is debilitating.

The time in between Jesus' death and resurrection must have been so painful, so dark, so heartbreaking, so catastrophic

for Jesus' family and friends. Grief. Disappointment. Guilt for some. Fear. Life trajectories changed overnight.

We lose loved ones, too. We lose jobs. Experience injuries. Sickness. Death. And we reel in the aftermath. Living on this side of history has its benefits, though. We will never experience a darkness so deep as those in-between hours—because Easter did happen.

The resurrection took place. The God who took on the filth of our sin is alive, returned to heaven, and has sent the Holy Spirit to us. Our Counselor. The one who teaches, instructs, and comforts our hearts. He convicts us of sin, draws us to himself, opens the scripture to our understanding, and guarantees our inheritance.

Nevertheless, I am telling you the truth. It is for your benefit that I go away, because if I don't go away the Counselor will not come to you. If I go, I will send him to you. (John 16:7)

But the Counselor, the Holy Spirit, whom the Father will send in my name, will teach you all things and remind you of everything I have told you. (John 14:26)

When he comes, he will convict the world about sin, righteousness, and judgment: About sin, because they do not believe in me; about righteousness, because I am going to the Father and you will no longer see me; and about judgment, because the ruler of this world has been judged. (John 16:8-11)

Will you experience grief? Yes. Confusion? Yes. Pain and loss? Yes and yes. This world can be a hard, hard place. But Jesus lives. And the Holy

I Have Received the Holy Spirit

Spirit lives in you. And you, therefore, have the power of God within you to meet those hard, hard moments, not alone, but with God present.

I have been crucified with Christ, and I no longer live, but Christ lives in me. The life I now live in the body, I live by faith in the Son of God, who loved me and gave himself for me. (Galatians 2:20)

Remember that when you became a Christian, your identity became forever bound up with Christ through the power of the Holy Spirit. Jesus is no longer dead. And you have the power of God inside you through the Holy Spirit.

The Holy Spirit is the most precious gift we'll ever receive. He helps, counsels, comforts, teaches, guides, enlightens, convicts, seals, encourages, exhorts, reveals truth, gives spiritual gifts, and produces spiritual fruit.

❈ How have you experienced the Holy Spirit in your life?

❈ What does his presence in your life say about who you are?

❈ Ask him to reveal himself in new or deeper ways to you today

I Have Received the Holy Spirit

Thank you, Father, for Easter. For the never-again-in-between hours. For the astonishing power and gift of the Holy Spirit. For the way he works in my heart to draw me ever deeper into a relationship with you, the way he helps me understand things of God, the way he works in my life to show more of you to the world. What a crazy-amazing gift, made possible by your resurrection and ascension. Thank you for being willing to endure what is to us a holy week, for being willing to endure physical death and the separation from God—for me. I revel in your resurrection, not only this weekend, but every moment of every day. Thank you for grace and hope. Spirit, help me understand more about who you are and how you work in my life. Help me honor you, listen to you, and obey you.

I love you. Amen.

WEEK 12
DAY 03

There's a backcountry survival memory device called the rule of three. It says that assuming the preceding items aren't a problem, that you can survive:

Three minutes without AIR.

Three hours without SHELTER.

Three days without WATER.

Three weeks without FOOD.[1]

It's not a hard-and-fast rule. There are too many variables to really predict how long any individual can survive without water in any given situation, for example. It's a memory trigger to help you prioritize your attention in a survival situation. We often think we need to secure food or water first, but exposure can put you in serious danger much faster than dehydration.

One of the most important skills needed for survival is learning to create a shelter from available materials. A shelter can protect from the weather and animals. It can make the difference between death from hypothermia and hugging your family again. Mental state is also critically important in a survival situation, and shelter is a powerful boost to emotional well-being.

We don't just need shelter in survival situations, though. It's considered a basic human

need. Spiritual shelter is important, too.

> The one who lives under the protection of the
> Most High
> dwells in the shadow of the Almighty.
> I will say concerning the Lord, who is my
> refuge and my fortress,
> my God in whom I trust:
> He himself will rescue you from the bird trap,
> from the destructive plague.
> He will cover you with his feathers;
> you will take refuge under his wings.
> His faithfulness will be a protective shield.
> You will not fear the terror of the night,
> the arrow that flies by day,
> the plague that stalks in darkness,
> or the pestilence that ravages at noon.
> (Psalm 91:1-6)

We dwell in his shadow. He is our refuge and fortress. He will rescue us. We can take cover in him. He is a protective shield. We need not fear. Such protective language! From the strength of a fortress, to the care of rescue from a trap, to the safety under his wings, we are assured that we are sheltered and need not fear.

Sooner or later in life you will feel trapped. You will face a storm. You will be exposed and vulnerable to attack. There will be terrors, arrows, plagues, or disease. When these things happen, we tend to look to friends, family, authorities, professionals, and organizations for protection, support, and care—and we should. Community is important, and we should take advantage of the resources that we've been given. But never forget that God is the most important shelter, provider, and protector that

we have. He will never fail you.

- These verses speak of God as a rescuer, a refuge, a fortress, a protector, a shield, and as sheltering wings. Which analogy speaks to you from these verses and why?
- We need not fear anything in the night or day. Why? What's the basis of our confidence?
- How do you need to respond today?

Father,

Thank you for your protection. Thank you for your strength, your care, your provision, your faithfulness, your power and love that gives me the knowledge that you can and will do what you've promised. Chase fear from my heart and let me stand confident in the face of dangers both real and imagined that I am sheltered by the Lord Almighty.

I love you. Amen.

WEEK 12
DAY 04

I have quirky eyes. I don't see quite like everyone else. When I was growing up, I occasionally noticed oddities in my sight. I couldn't see any difference when using 3D glasses and I had issues learning to drive. Sitting in a college psychology class as a freshman listening to a lecture on developmental psychology, I realized that my binocular depth perception never developed.

Most people understand distance and depth by the brain overlapping and interpreting images seen by both eyes. This is what creates binocular depth perception. This usually develops as a toddler, but my eyes weren't working together at that age—I was born with what's commonly called, "crossed eyes." I had surgery to correct most of it as a child, but not until after the stage when depth perception develops. So my eyes and brain don't work the way most people's do. I only have atmospheric cues for distance, like items are smaller the farther away they are. I suspect my world seems much less dimensional than yours does, but I have no way to know for sure.

Because of my inability to process depth information well, I'm a bit of a klutz. I tend to run into door jambs with my shoulders. Frequently.

I also trip over things. Even small things like completely imaginary items on the floor. It's so second nature at this point, that I'm constantly bruised from things I'm not even aware I've run into!

> Now to him who is able to protect you from stumbling and to make you stand in the presence of his glory, without blemish and with great joy. (Jude 1:24)

Spiritually, I often feel like a klutz, too. I don't put God first. I say things I shouldn't. I can be prideful, greedy, independent, self-serving, self-important, selfish—self, self, self. Do you detect a theme? I'm not alone in this, I know. We humans can't walk for more than a few moments of life without tripping over a sin. Spiritual stumbles are frequent and can be painful.

It's a good thing I don't have to rely on my own effort to keep from a serious stumble! We don't rely on our own righteousness. We don't rely on our own ability to stand in God's presence without blemish. Because of Christ, instead of the guilt and judgment we deserve, we stand in God's presence with great joy.

While we are soldiers, witnesses, salt, and light in our world—and those roles and responsibilities require effort on our part—God knows we're human. We won't be perfect. We won't follow perfectly. He knows we're prone to stumble. And he's got us. We need to seek him, persevere, grow in faith, and all the other things he instructs us to do, but even when we don't, he's able to protect us from stumbling. We do need to put effort into living a holy life—out of love and obedience, not as a way to gain approval—but

I Am Protected From Stumbling

ultimately our effort isn't what keeps us safe in God's hands. His effort is.

✤ How has God protected you from stumbling in the past?

✤ What things tend to spiritually trip you up?

✤ What actions do you need to take today?

Father,

Help me rely on your ability to keep me from stumbling, not my own effort. Teach me not to rely on myself. Open my eyes to times you've protected me in the past and let me remember those in the future and see them as evidence of your love for me. Teach me to recognize the things that trip me up and help me turn away from them. Thank you for the incredible privilege of being able to stand in your presence with joy. Unbelievable joy.

I love you. Amen.

WEEK 12
DAY 05

I have a friend who rented a storage unit for some spare furniture and boxes. Several months into his rental agreement, he arrived one weekend to drop off or pick up some things from his unit and discovered that the gate had been damaged. The gate typically lifts above the entering and exiting vehicles at the entrance to the business. But someone had misjudged the height of the gate and/or the height of the trailer they were towing and tried to drive through the gate before it was completely out of the way.

The gate's now out of commission.

If you read about my lack of depth perception and wonder if this is one more example of how my eyes can wreak havoc in my life, it's (thankfully) not. I wasn't even in the same state at the time. I promise!

The storage business has a problem. The gate was important. It protected the customers' things stored in those units. They've paid for the security that gate provided.

We want to guard and protect the things that are valuable to us.

You are being guarded by God's power through faith for a salvation that is ready to be

revealed in the last time. (1 Peter 1:5)

The word for "guarded" in this verse is "phroureo," and it's used four times in the New Testament. It's derived from a word meaning "sentinel." It has three primary nuances, but all have a military reference. In this verse, the sense is to provide security, guard, protect, or keep.[2]

Precept Austin shares a story "told of a Scotsman, who was typically economical, leaving instructions that only one word should be engraved upon his tombstone. That word taken from this verse was the single word KEPT (KJV translation). Eternal security is not based on the faith of men, but on the faithfulness of God."[3]

And who is doing the guarding? Psalm 121 says,

I lift my eyes toward the mountains.
Where will my help come from?
My help comes from the Lord,
the Maker of heaven and earth.
He will not allow your foot to slip;
your Protector will not slumber.
Indeed, the Protector of Israel
does not slumber or sleep.
The Lord protects you;
the Lord is a shelter right by your side.
The sun will not strike you by day
or the moon by night.
The Lord will protect you from all harm;
he will protect your life.
The Lord will protect your coming and going
both now and forever.

I Am Guarded

✚ You are guarded. What does this say about your identity?

✚ What is meaningful today to you about your guardian from Psalm 121?

✚ How should the answers to the two questions above impact your actions or attitudes?

Father,

You are the maker of heaven and earth. You do not sleep; you are always watching out for me. You are a shelter by my side. You protect me at all times in all places. You find me worthy of constant care and protection. Thank you. Help me understand how valuable I am. Help me live my life in a way that flows from that understanding.

I love you. Amen.

WEEK 12
DAY 06

When we were kids, we played hide and seek. You know how to play, right? One player hides their eyes and counts while all the others scramble to find themselves a hiding place. The one counting then looks for the other players. When they find one, that person becomes the seeker. In my family, we preferred a variation where one person hid, and all the rest searched. As each person found the one hiding, they squeezed (or tried to squeeze) into the hiding spot alongside those already there. The squeezing into (or inability to squeeze into) the hiding spots increased the fun factor dramatically.

When you're playing hide and seek, no one wanders off and leaves the hidden friends hidden. Even dinner bells are ignored until the game is over.

So if you have been raised with Christ, seek the things above, where Christ is, seated at the right hand of God. Set your minds on things above, not on earthly things. For you died, and your life is hidden with Christ in God. (Colossians 3:1-3)

In this verse, the word "hidden" indicates

something accomplished in the past with permanent results. This game doesn't end and our hiding spot is permanently ours. Our lives have been hidden in Christ forever. No seeker is going to come and expose us. No one is going to call time and kick us out of our hiding spot. Our life has been hidden in Christ and will always stay hidden in him. It was accomplished in the past with permanent results.

In Colossians 3 and 4, Paul is essentially telling us that we should live out what God has done for us. We shouldn't just intellectually understand the positional, legal, and spiritual truths that we've been absorbing throughout this book. Our understanding should affect our behavior, attitudes, habits, actions, and conversations. Our position should change our practice.

I once spent a summer in Florida and visited Tarpon Springs with a friend. This bustling little town on the Gulf of Mexico is known for two things: having the highest concentration of Greek Americans in the United States and sponge diving. Wikipedia says, "In 1905, John Cocoris introduced the technique of sponge diving to Tarpon Springs by recruiting divers and crew members from Greece... The sponge industry soon became one of the leading maritime industries in Florida and the most important business in Tarpon Springs, generating millions of dollars a year."[4]

Sponge diving is the oldest known form of underwater diving and was originally performed as free diving. Divers used a heavy rock to get them to the bottom quickly, then held their breath while collecting sponges from the ocean floor.[5] But by the time the industry was booming in Tarpon Springs, divers put on heavy diving

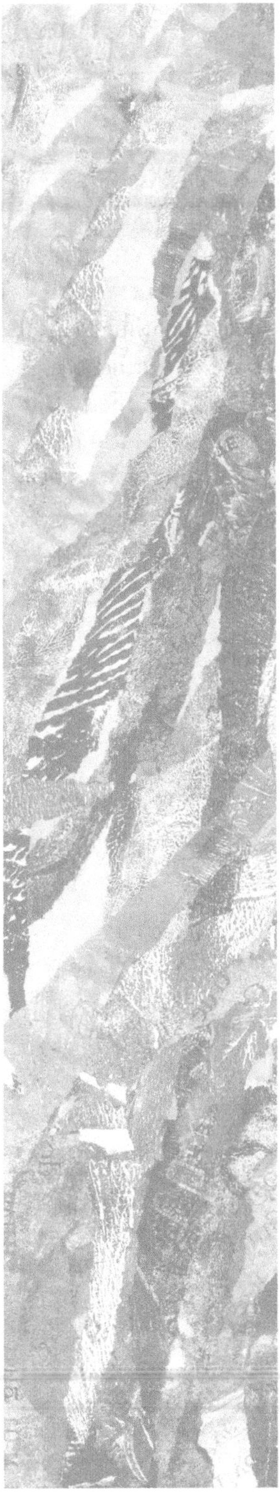

gear, walked the seabed collecting sponges, and breathed through a hose connected to a tank on the boat. They were tethered to the boat while walking the floor of the gulf.

This boat-based air source was unseen on board the boat above them, but absolutely critical to their survival. Your life has been changed by your belief that Jesus took the punishment for your sins, died, and was resurrected. The trajectory of your forever future was altered in the moment you recognized and accepted that sacrifice on your behalf. In that moment, the things we've been studying became reality for you. You became an adopted child of the king. You became complete in Christ. You became one of God's children, a chosen, treasured, loved, dependent friend of Jesus. Your life has been hidden forever in Christ.

But how you practice that reality in your own circumstances is up to you. The way that happens is by living your life tethered to God, like the Tarpon Springs divers paced the sea bottom linked to the life-giving air on their boats. You need to breathe in the Word and presence of God daily. And you need to act on the truths of who God says you are.

- What does your being hidden in Christ permanently mean for you?
- What is one step you can take today to make your position in Christ more evident in your life?

I Am Hidden

Father,

I know I am safe in your care. I know that having been hidden in you, I will always be hidden in you. Help me learn to rely on you for life. Help me constantly refocus my attention on spiritual realities and prioritize them over earthly things. Train my heart, my mind, my attention to be on things above. Sink the truths deeply into my heart of who you say I am and let my heart, thoughts, actions, and attitudes be transformed by them.

I love you. Amen.

WEEK 12
DAY 07

This week, we looked at how God is looking out for us. We understand that we've received the Holy Spirit and we're sheltered, guarded, protected, and hidden.

What has God spoken to your heart this week?

How have these truths changed the way you think or feel about yourself?

Father,

Thank you for all the truths of scripture you've given me to know who I am. Continue to grow my understanding of my identity. Continue to speak to me about how you've created me. Continue to grow my faith, my knowledge, and my obedience. Draw me more and more deeply into a relationship with you. May my life bring you glory and fame everywhere I am. May my heart treasure the truths of your Word, and may my life fulfill the purposes you intend.

I love you. Amen.

NOW WHAT

What's your next step? Maybe you want to continue to spend time with God daily, but you need some guidance. Or, maybe you don't have time to deal with figuring out how or what to do. Maybe it's just easier to follow instructions. Or, maybe you have trouble being consistent and following through (Hello, this is SO me!).

I have a solution for you!

I offer a daily guide to help you spend time with God on a consistent basis. It's a short audio file published each weekday, guiding you through a time of connecting with God in scripture and personal prayer. You can listen on any device at whatever time and place you find convenient. Then, join us in a private community to talk about what God said to you in your time with him.

As one of my readers, you can receive a free sample week of this service!

Have you ever wondered, "If God has all things under his control, knows all things, and can do whatever he wants (according to his nature), why do I need to pray?" We'll answer that question in this free sample series! Go to **www.whogodsaysyouare.link/whypray** to get started!

THANK YOU FOR READING!

Did you enjoy this book? Consider sharing it with others!

One of the best ways to support authors and help more people find books you like is to write a quick review on Amazon. It doesn't have to be long or complicated, just a quick sentence telling others what you enjoyed most about the book. Reviews will significantly impact the number of people who are exposed to the book.

It's really easy! Go to amazon.com and find the book by searching "Who God Says You Are." When you reach the book page, scroll down to the Customer Review section and click the "Write a Customer Review" button. Enter the information, and there you have it! You've given me an early birthday present! Thanks, you're awesome!

Other ways you can share:

+ Share or mention the book on your social media platforms. Include the hashtag #whogodsaysyouare so we can see it too!

+ Recommend this book for your church, book club, small group, or class.

+ Gift the book to family or friends who would find it helpful.

Thanks again for your support!

NOTES

Week 1 | What's the foundation of who I am?

1. Tackett, Del. "What's A Christian Worldview?" Focus On The Family, https://www.focusonthefamily.com/faith/christian-worldview/whats-a-christian-worldview/whats-a-worldview-anyway.
2. As calculated at the time of publication at https://data.bls.gov/cgi-bin/cpicalc.pl.

Week 2 | What's the legal basis for who I am?

1. Wikipedia. "Larry Nassar," Wikipedia.com, https://en.wikipedia.org/wiki/Larry_Nassar.
2. The Guardian. "How was Larry Nassar able to abuse so many gymnasts for so long?", January 26, 2018, theguardian.com, https://www.theguardian.com/sport/2018/jan/26/larry-nassar-abuse-gymnasts-scandal-culture.
3. Piper, John. "Free from Sin, Slaves of Righteousness, Part 2," Desiring God, December 3, 2000, https://www.desiringgod.org/messages/free-from-sin-slaves-of-righteousness-part-2.
4. Got Questions. "What is sanctification? What is the definition of Christian sanctification?" GotQuestions.org, https://www.gotquestions.org/sanctification.html.

Week 3 | What's my relationship status? Part 2

1. Wike, Richard. "5 ways Americans and Europeans are different," Pew Research Center, April 19, 2018, http://www.pewresearch.org/fact-tank/2016/04/19/5-ways-americans-and-europeans-are-different/.
2. Guillebeau, Chris. "What Does Independence Mean To You?" chrisguillebeau.com, July 2012, https://chrisguillebeau.com/what-does-independence-mean/.
3. TheRomantic.com. "ABIGAIL ADAMS TO JOHN ADAMS – DEC 23, 1782," theromantic.com, http://theromantic.com/LoveLetters/adams.htm.
4. PBS. "The Emperor and Empress," pbs.org, https://www.pbs.org/empires/napoleon/n_josephine/emperor/page_1.html.
5. Wellesnet: the orson welles web resource. "Orson Welles to Rita Hayworth: "You are my life – my very life." wellesnet.com, February 27, 2010, http://www.wellesnet.com/orson-welles-to-rita-hayworth-you-are-my-life-my-very-life/.
6. Aguillard, Anna. "11 Reasons Why Johnny and June Are #RelationshipGoals," Southern Living, https://www.southernliving.com/culture/celebrities/johnny-cash-june-carter-relationship. Bonus: You can see an image of the note at

this site in addition to the article.

7. Esquivel, Paloma. "Richard Nixon's love letters to wife Pat go on display," Los Angeles Times, March 13, 2012, http://latimesblogs.latimes.com/la-now/2012/03/richard-nixons-love-letters-to-wife-patricia-go-on-display.html

8. Piper, John. "Ten Reasons to Revel in Being Chosen," Desiring God, October 27, 2015, https://www.desiringgod.org/articles/ten-reasons-to-revel-in-being-chosen.

9. Waters, TaMaryn. "Lost & Found: Baby Charlie is couple's Christmas miracle," Tallahassee Democrat, December 23, 2017, https://www.tallahassee.com/story/news/2017/12/23/lost-found-baby-charlie-couples-christmas-miracle/948593001/.

10. Ibid.

11. Unicef. "Orphans," unicef.org, https://www.unicef.org/media/orphans.

12. International Labour Organization. "Child Labour," ilo.org, https://www.ilo.org/global/topics/child-labour/lang--en/index.htm.

13. World Health Organization. "Malnutrition," who.int, February 16, 2018, http://www.who.int/news-room/fact-sheets/detail/malnutrition.

14. UNICEF. "More than 16 million babies born into conflict this year: UNICEF" unicef.org, December 17, 2015, https://www.unicef.org/png/media_25015.html.

Week 4 | What's my relationship status? Part 2

1. Howard, Kathy. "You are a Princess!" kathyhoward.org, October 25, 2012, https://www.kathyhoward.org/you-are-a-princess/.

2. Google Dictionary. "Saint," google.com, https://www.google.com/search?q=saint+definition&oq=saint+definition&aqs=chrome..69i57j69i60l-3j0l2.2531j1j4&sourceid=chrome&ie=UTF-8.

3. Saunders, William. "The Process of Becoming a Saint," Catholic Education Resource Center, https://www.catholiceducation.org/en/culture/catholic-contributions/the-process-of-becoming-a-saint.html.

4. Bridges, Jerry. Who Am I? - Identity in Christ. Adelphi: Cruciform Press, 2012.

Week 5 | Where am I and why does it matter?

1. Kleon, Austin. Steal Like An Artist, New York: Workman. 2012.

2. Bos, Carole. "Abe Lincoln with His Son Tad" AwesomeStories.com. Jun 04, 2014. Oct 15, 2018, http://www.awesomestories.com/asset/view/Abe-Lincoln-with-His-Son-Tad1.

3. Wright, Samuel. "Plato and Soul Mates," Brigham Young University, https://humanities.byu.edu/plato-and-soul-mates/.

Week 6 | What is my spiritual identity?

1. UsingEnglish.com. "What does 'Bless your pointy little head' mean?" usingenglish.com, https://www.usingenglish.com/reference/idioms/bless-+your+pointy+little+head.html.

2. The Free Dictionary by Farlex. "bless the world with (one's) heels," idioms.thefreedictionary.com, https://idioms.thefreedictionary.com/bless+the+world+with+your+heels.

3. The Free Dictionary by Farlex. "bless (one's) cotton socks," idioms.thefreedictionary.com, https://idioms.thefreedictionary.com/Bless+cotton+socks.

4. Howard, Kathy. "Every Spiritual Blessing - Ephesians 1:1-14," kathyhoward.org, January 25, 2012, https://www.kathyhoward.org/every-spiritual-blessing-ephesians-1-1-1/.

5. GotQuestions. "What are spiritual blessings?" gotquestions.com, https://www.gotquestions.org/spiritual-blessings.html.

6. Bragg, Rick. All Over But the Shoutin'. New York: Vintage, 1998.

7. Bragg, Rick. My Southern Journey. New York: Time Inc. Books, 2015.

8. Dailey, Jim. "The Reality of Spiritual Warfare," billygraham.org, January 24, 2005, https://billygraham.org/decision-magazine/february-2005/the-reality-of-spiritual-warfare/.

9. Piper, John. "Sealed by the Spirit to the Day of Redemption." Desiring God, May 6, 1984, https://www.desiringgod.org/messages/sealed-by-the-spirit-to-the-day-of-redemption.

Week 7 | How does God describe me?

1. The Diamond Loupe. "Average Engagement Ring Spend in 2017 (in US): $6,351," thediamondloupe.com, November 20. 2017, https://www.thediamondloupe.com/articles/2017-11-20/average-engagement-ring-spend-2017-us-6351.

2. Wikipedia. "Cullinan Diamond," wikipedia.com, https://en.wikipedia.org/wiki/Cullinan_Diamond.

3. Historic Royal Palaces. "The Crown Jewels," hrp.org.uk, https://www.hrp.org.uk/tower-of-london/history-and-stories/the-crown-jewels/#gs._iTIxh8.

4. Wikipedia. "Cullinan Diamond," wikipedia.com, https://en.wikipedia.org/wiki/Cullinan_Diamond.

5. Worthy. "The Cullinan Diamond," worthy.com, https://www.worthy.com/famous-diamonds/the-cullinan-diamond

6. Carson, D.A. "Why We Must Understand the Temple in God's Plan Today," Desiring God, July 22, 2015, https://www.desiringgod.org/interviews/why-we-must-understand-the-temple-in-gods-plan-today.

7. Wikipedia. "Great Chicago Fire," wikipedia.com, https://en.wikipedia.org/wiki/Great_Chicago_Fire.

8. Ibid.

9. Wikipedia. " Fire Whirl," wikipedia.com, https://en.wikipedia.org/wiki/Fire_whirl.

10. Ibid.

11. Ibid.

12. Chicago - Architecture & Cityscape. "Seven buildings that survived the Great Chicago Fire of 1871." chicago-architecture-jyoti.blogspot.com, February 21, 2009, http://chicago-architecture-jyoti.blogspot.com/2009/02/six-survivors-of-great-chicago-fire-of.html.

13. Wikipedia. "Great Chicago Fire," wikipedia.com, https://en.wikipedia.org/wiki/Great_Chicago_Fire.

Week 8 | What is spiritual citizenship and why should I care?

1. Piper, John. "Children, Heirs, and Fellow Sufferers," Desiring God, April 21, 2002, https://www.desiringgod.org/messages/children-heirs-and-fellow-sufferers.

2. Wikipedia. "Round Table," wikipedia.com, https://en.wikipedia.org/wiki/Round_Table.

3. Mullen, Jethro. "Poised for attack: Photo shows lion shortly before mauling woman to death," Cable News Network, June 9, 2015, https://www.cnn.com/2015/06/08/world/africa-lion-attack-photo/index.html.

4. Ibid.

5. Lion Alert. "Let's Look at Lions," lionalert.org, http://lionalert.org/page/Lets_look_at_lions.

6. Starr, Lois Anne. "Can a lion licj your skin off?" Quora, https://www.quora.com/Can-a-lion-lick-your-skin-off.

7. Wikipedia. "Lion," wikipedia.com, https://en.wikipedia.org/wiki/Lion.

Week 9 | What does God say about my purpose?

1. Wikipedia. "Salting (food)," wikipedia.com, https://en.wikipedia.org/wiki/Salting_(food).

2. Seametrics. "100 Amazing Water Facts You Should Know," seametrics.com, https://www.seametrics.com/blog/water-facts/.

3. Ibid.

4. Ibid.

5. Ibid.

6. Ibid.

Week 10 | What's the result of my identity?

1. Lewis, Zoe. "Zoe Lewis-Sheep". YouTube video, 3:32. Posted December 22, 2013. https://www.youtube.com/watch?v=2-rJIW_6Bfc/.

2. Heitzig, Skip. "The Good Shepherd and His Happy Sheep," Billy Graham Evangelistic Association, October 28, 2012, https://billygraham.org/decision-magazine/october-2012/the-good-shepherd-and-his-happy-sheep/.

3. stuka370. "Soldiers of reddit, what is combat really like? And Does the media do it justice?" reddit.com, January 24, 2013, https://www.reddit.com/r/AskReddit/comments/1782zv/soldiers_of_reddit_what_is_combat_really_like_and/.

4. Benjamin Franklin Historical Society. "Ambassador to France," benjamin-franklin-history.org, http://www.benjamin-franklin-history.org/ambassador-to-france/.

5. PBS. "Benjamin Franklin, 1779 Minister to France," pbs.org, https://www.pbs.org/benfranklin/l3_world_france.html.

6. Returning the Favor. "Adah's Dirty Laundry," web series, April 23, 2018, https://www.facebook.com/ReturningTheFavor/videos/adahs-dirty-laundry/2056004218004171/.

Week 11 | What truths does God want me to believe?

1. Piper, John. "How Do You Press On to Make It Your Own?" Desiring God, March 14, 2007, https://www.desiringgod.org/articles/how-do-you-press-on-to-make-it-your-own.

Week 12 | How secure is my identity?

1. Backcountry Chronicles. "Wilderness Survival Rules of 3 – Air, Shelter, Water and Food," backcountrychronicles.com, http://www.backcountry-chronicles.com/wilderness-survival-rules-of-3/.

2. Precept Austin. "1 Peter 1:5 Commentary," preceptaustin.org, March 6, 2017, https://www.preceptaustin.org/1_peter_15.

3. Ibid.

4. Wikipedia. "Tarpon Springs, Florida," wikipedia.com, https://en.wikipedia.org/wiki/Tarpon_Springs,_Florida.

5. Wikipedia. "Sponge Diving," wikipedia.com, https://en.wikipedia.org/wiki/Sponge_diving.

ACKNOWLEDGEMENTS

I now understand the dilemma recipients have when they stand up to accept an award. We live in a complex, interconnected web of relationships. Who we are and what we do is so connected to what others have contributed to our lives that it's impossible to take credit for doing something alone and impossible to acknowledge all those who should be thanked.

I'm incredibly grateful for any of you who have poured into my life over the years. For this project, special thanks and my deepest gratitude goes out to:

My parents and family for being ridiculously supportive and encouraging.

My son for inspiring me to be a better person.

My cheerleader friends who never fail to make me feel like I can climb impossible mountains: Shea Williams, Tim Hill, and Margie Schulz. Hugs and high fives all around. Y'all are some of God's best gifts to me!

My accountability partner, Dania Demirci, for keeping me on track, moving forward, and looking toward Christ. Thank you for speaking just the right words exactly when I need them.

My prayer warrior, Dee Bradford, for helping give these words and my efforts power they wouldn't otherwise have.

My production team: Marcy Pusey for coaching and advice, Arlene Berkey and Wandering Words Media for editing, and Shea Williams for interior design and formatting.

My Bridge community group 2017-18 for whom these words were originally written. Your diving in, wrestling with, and discussing

these topics with vulnerability and bravery was so moving, gratifying, and inspiring to me. Thank you for the constant encouragement and for the initial—and repeated—requests that these words be published.

And last, but most importantly, thank you Jesus, for being the living Word, for giving authors words which have enriched my life so often, and for giving these particular words to me. May they find a home in hungry hearts, provide a clearer understanding of who you created us to be, and draw people into a deeper relationship with you.

Who God Says Women Are

A second book in the *Who God Says You Are* series.

ABOUT THE AUTHOR

Michelle has been in church leadership for much of the last twenty years and currently serves as a volunteer staff member at The Bridge, a church Outreach Magazine named the fifth fastest-growing church in America in 2018.

She thinks living outside of Nashville, Tennessee with her son, her sometimes-crazy Boxer dog, too many art supplies, and an overwhelming number of ideas is great if you love hot chicken, creativity, and humidity.

Well, two out of three ain't bad.

Find out more and connect with Michelle at **www.graceandthegravelroad.com.**

Soli Deo gloria

Made in the USA
Middletown, DE
30 August 2019